D1077000

Navigating Complexity

"A... ...ellent, easy-to-read overview."

New Scientist magazine

"Navigating Complexity contains ideas to provoke, challenge and stimulate those working at senior levels in any role. Battram has taken a huge amount of source material and put it into a form where it can (and should!) be used by innovative managers and consultants. He has done a splendid job of bringing together the different aspects of complexity into a single, excellently laid out volume. This book should find a place in the library of any leader, strategist or consultant who likes to create their own models and methods by synthesising ideas rather than following someone else's recipe."

Long Range Planning, the Strategic Planning Society journal

"The best designed and best illustrated of all the complexity and management books. More than just another 'how-to' book , this is a 'how-to-think' book for practising managers. Within this book lies the craft of management. Armed with the concepts herein, the manager of today is better prepared to face the complexities of tomorrow. Without such mastery, the risk is chaos and confusion."

Michael Lissack,
Editor-in-Chief, *Emergence: A Journal of Complexity Issues in Organizations and Management*
Director, The Networking, Emergence and Complexity Studies Initiative

---

"Presents concepts of complexity theory in a structured, well illustrated and direct way which is anything but complex."

Management Skills & Development magazine

"He has grasped a wide variety of concepts from many contemporary fields and made them accessible and useful for executives and managers. Breakthroughs in results will occur if they are taken on board."

Michael McMaster, Director, Knowledge Based Development Ltd, and author of *The Intelligence Advantage*

"Essential reading for every manager in local government who wants to bring about creative change."

Tony Bovaird, Director, Public Sector Management Research Centre, Aston Business School

---

"For me it is the key reference guide to this crucial area of management theory."

Nick Zeniuk, co-developer of the Team Learning Lab with Fred Simon and Peter Senge

---

"A writer and consultant with a profound understanding of complexity and its applications."

Roger Lewin, author of *Complexity: Life at the Edge of Chaos*

"Short comprehensible chapters doing just what he promises – taking the interested manager (or other amateur 'nexialist') on a guided tour of the field, from fractals to factories. It requires no maths background, but teaches you how to think about complex issues in today's ways."

Jack Cohen, co-author, with Ian Stewart, of *The Collapse of Chaos*

"A powerful guide to thinking and managing your way into the new economy."

Charles Leadbeater, author of *Living on Thin Air: the New Economy*.

Navigating Complexity

The Essential Guide to Complexity Theory in Business and Management

Arthur Battram

The Industrial Society

OXSTALLS LEARNING CENTRE
UNIVERSITY OF GLOUCESTERSHIRE
Oxstalls Lane
Gloucester GL2 9HW
Tel: 01452 876685

Navigating Complexity is based on *The Complexicon: a Lexicon of Complexity* originally published in 1996 by The Local Government Management Board (LGMB) as part of its *Learning from Complexity* pack.

This paperback edition first published by The Industrial Society in 1999
Reprinted January 2001

Navigating Complexity was first published in 1998 by
The Industrial Society
Robert Hyde House
48 Bryanston Square
London W1H 7LN
Telephone: +44 (0)20 7479 2136

© Arthur Battram

ISBN 1 85835 870 1

Industrial Society
Business Books Network
163 Central Avenue
Suite 2
Hopkins Professional Building
Dover
NH 03820
USA

British Library Cataloguing-in-Publication Data.
A catalogue record for this book is available from the
British Library.

Library of congress Cataloguing-in-Publication Data on File.

All rights reserved. No part of this publication may be reproduced, stored in a retrieval system or transmitted, in any form or by any means, electronic, mechanical, photocopying, recording and/or otherwise without the prior written permission of the publishers. This book may not be lent, resold, hired out or otherwise disposed of by way of trade in any form, binding or cover other than that in which it is published, without prior consent of the publishers.

Arthur Battram asserts his moral right to be identified as the author of this work.

Printed by: J. W. Arrowsmith Ltd

Designed by: C3

Cover design by: C3

Cover illustration by: Michael Edwards

Page 262 is given with permission for the reader to photocopy

The Industrial Society is a Registered Charity No. 290003

ref 1488tw1.01

For my father, a creative engineer, for teaching me how to think.
To my mother for bringing forth my world.
To Sarah, my muse.

Acknowledgements

Major contributions by Steve Trivett

Edited by Andrew Kelsey and Arthur Battram

Final draft readers and advisers: Sarah Ashby, Mark McKergow, Steve Trivett. For the Industrial Society: Sheridan Maguire, Susannah Lear

Format devised by Arthur Battram and designed by by C3, Cambridge

Grateful thanks are given to The Local Government Management Board for permission to reprint portions of *The Complexicon: a Lexicon of Complexity* from the *Learning from Complexity* pack published by the LGMB

Viking and Oxford University Press for permission to use text and illustrations from *At Home in the Universe* by Stuart Kauffman. Copyright 1995 by Stuart Kauffman. Used by permission of Oxford University Press, Inc

Michael McMaster, Knowledge Based Development Ltd, for email dialogue and permission to use copyright material posted to the Learning Organisation email discussion group and taken from his book *The Intelligence Advantage*

John Darwin, Sheffield Business School, for permission to quote from his unpublished paper *The Wisdom Paradigm* in the entries for 'complex adaptive systems' and 'perspectives'

Michael Lissack, for permission to quote from his unpublished paper *Chaos and Complexity: What does that have to do with Management?*, in the 'fitness landscape' entry

Berrett-Koehler, for permission to quote from *Leadership and the New Science: Learning about Organisation from a Disorderly Universe*, copyright 1994 by Margaret Wheatley. Berrett-Koehler Publishers, Inc, San Francisco, CA. All rights reserved

Abacus and W. H. Freeman and Company for permission to use text and illustration from *The Quark and the Jaguar: Adventures in the Simple and the Complex* by Murray Gell-Mann. Copyright 1994 by Murray Gell-Mann. Used by permission of W. H. Freeman and Company

Kevin Kelly, for permission to quote from his book *Out of Control: the New Biology of Machines*, Fourth Estate, 1994

Foreword

This is a novel book, presented in a novel way, about an intriguing and increasingly pivotal subject.

Twentieth century organisations wrestled with how to make hierarchical, `command and control', managerial systems effective in a complex environment - by the last decade of the century experimentation was underway. Traditional management approaches no longer performed adequately, and companies and public agencies alike looked to more democratic, open and networking styles of management. Even those that had mixed success knew that a different direction was needed; in today's highly competitive environment organisations need to tap every possible source of creativity, intelligence and loyalty. Above all, managerial legitimacy has to be earned every working day of every working week.

In this book, Arthur Battram offers a route map to the concepts and theorems that will undoubtedly inform management styles in the twenty-first century.
He does not supply answers; rather he describes an approach. To navigate complexity, he argues, we have to learn to listen, to delegate, to network and build relationships; and this demands a reinvention of how managers manage, and what it means to lead an organisation.

It is an unsettling read, and if sometimes his book begs questions, it is an important and creative contribution to a debate that is set to continue. Everybody will profit one way or another from engaging with Battram's thesis. These are complex times, and the construction of a managerial response is one of the challenges of the new century. Read it.

Will Hutton
Chief Executive (designate), The Industrial Society

Contents

Using this book

 A specific reference to another entry within the book, e.g. the 'edge of chaos'.

In some instances you are referred to a specific paragraph within the entry, e.g. evolution of co-operation (entry)/the 'prisoner's dilemma' (paragraph).

Each entry is divided into the following parts:

Relevance
Indicates the relevance of the complexity idea to management theory and practice

Translation
Explores the complexity concept and its new language

Application
Examines the application of the ideas to the work of organisations

Cross-references
Lists additional cross-references to other items within the book

References
Indicates references to items not included in the book

Navigating complexity

> *"Complexity refers to the condition of the universe which is integrated and yet too rich and varied for us to understand in simple common mechanistic or linear ways. We can understand many parts of the universe in these ways but the larger and more intricately related phenomena can only be understood by principles and patterns – not in detail. Complexity deals with the nature of emergence, innovation, learning and adaptation."*
>
> Santa Fé Group, 1996

What happens when theory meets the real world?

Tom Peters tells us that the 'real' decisions aren't made in the boardroom the way the consultants would have it, but in the corridors outside, or over coffee. For most of us, the real world of work is total chaos: the phones never stop ringing and we just don't have time for yet another new theory. Wouldn't it be nice if the academics gave us something different; something to help us make sense of the mess we're in, instead of offering us more quick fixes? Management theory has a tradition of borrowing ideas from science in its search for the latest solution, but that's **not** what we're offering here. **Instead, we propose that you make up your own mind**.

Navigating Complexity brings you 20 of the key concepts that are transforming the way business people, scientists, and consultants think about what we call 'the real world'. Some of our most cherished management concepts are overturned in the process. To see what we mean check out the list overleaf:

increasing returns and lock-in

- *the economy will **never** reach equilibrium, the market does **not** know best*

 increasing returns and lock-in

- *knowledge **cannot** be managed like commodities because it can create more of itself, for almost nothing – like computer software*

 the 'edge of chaos', network and hierarchy

- *ordered systems **do not** collapse into chaos if left alone*

 perspectives/rationality

- *people **do not** behave rationally in their economic choices*

 ecosystem

- *it is **impossible** to assign clear boundaries to systems like nations, multinational companies or local government organisations*

 self-organisation

- ***nobody** is in charge of the Internet*

 memes

- *ideas spread **not** by rational thought, but by fashion and fads*

 metaphor, ecosystem

- *biological metaphors **not** machine metaphors are the starting point for engaging with our new world reality.*

What's interesting about this list is this: **you already know most of it**. Very little of it will come as a surprise to you, because you live and work in the real world, where these are the realities of human systems.

A new science that studies 95% of the real world

Unlike traditional science, which studies simple 'ideal' phenomena based on 'perfect laws' which can only be applied to a very narrow range of conditions, complexity theory studies the other 95%. These are the rules underlying the complex phenomena most common in the real world – effects like turbulence, disequilibrium and unpredictability, self-organisation, adaptation, learning, increasing returns and persistence. Complexity theory offers a range of new insights into the behaviour of social and economic systems. There are profound implications for learning, teamwork, partnership working, service delivery, quality approaches, change management, and policy and strategy implementation. But this isn't a new template for a new scientific management, because one of the fundamentals of the new 'complexity perspective' is that there are no right answers, no 'best' ways and no 'privileged' 'objective' viewpoints. Complexity theory both highlights the limits of our present approaches and offers a new perspective in which relationships and patterns are the new principles of organisation.

We can learn from science

We are now at a point where suddenly, after three hundred years of reductionism, most of which failed to say anything very useful about the realities of work in organisations, there is once again much to learn from science. The presence of science books in the best-seller listings for weeks at a time confirms this. Here, in *Navigating Complexity*, you will find a summary of the key ideas which are transforming the way we view the management of organisations.

But there are no easy answers this time

Society tends to listen to science when there is a crisis. The rise of 'agri-business' (the process by which farming became factory farming and agriculture turned our fields into industrial estates) is the result of governments saying to scientists, give us more food! This time it must be different: we cannot afford to ignore science because it is transforming our world and our relationship to it, but neither must we naively accept its conclusions as if they carry some kind of moral force. Science can enrich our understanding of our complex world but it cannot tell us right from wrong.

We are all part of the problem: are you part of the solution?
If there is one key message in complexity science, it is this: proceed cautiously.

Tiny 'insignificant' changes may be transforming your environment even as your latest change initiative is fizzling out. When everything is connected to everything else in an emergent pattern of possibilities, we are truly responsible for creating our shared future.

> "In our past explorations, the tradition was to discover something and then formulate it into answers and solutions that could be widely transferred. But now we are on a journey of mutual and simultaneous exploration. We cannot expect answers. Solutions, as quantum reality teaches, are temporary events, specific to a context, developed through the relationship of persons and circumstances. In this new world, you and I make it up as we go along, not because we lack expertise or planning skills, but because that is the nature of reality. Reality changes shape and meaning because of our activity. And it is constantly new. We are required to be there, as active participants. It can't happen without us and nobody can do it for us."

Margaret Wheatley

 References

Margaret Wheatley, *Leadership and the New Science: Learning about Organisation from a Disorderly Universe*, Berrett-Koehler, 1994, ISBN 1 881052 44 3

The format: a guidebook for travellers in complexity

Navigating Complexity is a reference work. Think of it as a 'Rough Guide to Complexity': it will give you an excellent background knowledge of the places you are preparing to visit, warn you of the dangers, and direct you to the most interesting places to experience. It won't teach you the whole language, just a few basic phrases to help you get started. It won't take you on a guided tour, or explain the mysterious customs and folkways of this enchanting country. What is on offer is signposting in the form of references at the end of each section. You can also update these information resources by visiting the *Navigating Complexity* website at:

www.indsoc.co.uk/navcom

New landscapes, new language

The metaphor of 'learning a new language when visiting a new country' has been chosen to emphasise that the key contribution of complexity theory is in **changing the way we talk about the world**, in order to change the way we see the world.

> *"... when a CEO wants to transform a company, he or she must first change the language of that company."*

> *"Our greatest obstacle in exploring ideas of complexity and complex systems is that we do not experience our world as occurring in language. For us, the world just 'is'. And the way it 'just is' is the way in which our language of linear, materialistic systems represents it to us."*
>
> Michael McMaster

The old problems are locked into the old language, and this applies to everyone involved in change, not just to senior management. If the language we use doesn't change, the things we do won't change. This book is therefore full of new language and new concepts designed to help you open up new perspectives and create new possibilities for change.

About the classification system
Navigating Complexity is organised into four main sections. There is a certain logic to this arrangement, but we must first take note of the words of that master of South American philosophical surrealism, Jorge Luis Borges, as quoted by Kevin Kelly:

> *"In an ancient Chinese encyclopaedia, the 'Celestial Emporium of Benevolent Knowledge', the categorisation scheme for animals was as follows: those that belong to the Emperor, embalmed ones, those that are trained, suckling pigs, mermaids, fabulous ones, stray dogs, those that are included in this classification, those that tremble as if they are mad, innumerable ones, those drawn with a very fine camel's hair brush, others, those that resemble flies from a distance."*

As Kelly says, far-fetched as the Celestial Emporium is, any classification scheme has its logical problems, and the one adopted here is no exception. It is possible to arrange the entries in this book in many different ways: much of the material in the 'Complex Behaviour' section could just as well be placed in 'The Web of Life'; equally the reader may rightly wonder why the entry on 'self-organisation' does not appear under 'The Patterns of Organisation' section. It is possible to justify almost any system of organisation when the subject is complexity theory – the aspects of which are inter-connected and inter-related by their very nature.

Where to start: a suggestion

Having made that clear, why have sections at all? Simply to 'chunk' the material so it is less daunting. Instead of reading an epic novel you are invited to read a collection of short stories. It is entirely up to the reader which entries are read in which order, except for one suggestion.

It may be useful to read section 1, 'The Patterns of Organisation', first as it contains much background material common to many of the other sections.

The entries

Each entry within a section has a related **graphic** together with a summary of the **relevance** of the idea, an explication of the idea and its **translation** into management theory and its **application**.

The sections

Each of the sections has its own introduction, in which the contents are listed and briefly discussed and their relevance explained. The four sections are:

Section 1: The Patterns of Organisation

The title refers to the shape of events and the processes that create, maintain and change them, rather than the structures of buildings or personnel charts. 'Organisation' as a verb, not a noun. In this section, several key ideas are introduced which underpin much of the rest of the book: the nature of systems, the effects of complexity, the crucial insights we can gain from studying complex adaptive systems and a new view of two old ideas, the hierarchy and the network.

Section 2: Landscapes of Possibility

This section focuses on the necessary learning, communication and possibility without which we cannot hope to cope with complexity. Using dialogue and metaphor, we can walk the landscapes of possibility, examining our world from many different perspectives, searching out creative solutions to complex problems.

Section 3: Complex Behaviour

'Complex behaviour' refers to the often paradoxical and surprising behaviour of simple-seeming systems governed by simple rules. In this section we examine the forces that operate to produce a kind of stability in complex systems. Computer simulation sits in the background of several of the entries in this section: computers are a key tool of complexity scientists. Several fondly held notions about change and change management are shown to be either erroneous or at best of limited use.

Section 4: The Web of Life

The 'web of life' represents the interconnectedness that is perhaps the most striking and perplexing feature of living systems – the most complex systems in the universe. The interplay of agents in competition with each other creates the environments in which improvements continually evolve, in which organisms and organisations seek to preserve themselves against a background of constant change.

References

Kevin Kelly, *Out of Control: the New Biology of Machines*, Fourth Estate, 1994, ISBN 1 85702 308 0

Michael McMaster, *The Intelligence Advantage: Organising for Complexity*, Butterworth-Heinemann, 1996, ISBN 0 7506 9792 X

About the author

Arthur Battram is a thinker, writer and consultant in the fields of change, knowledge and participation. His work with teams focuses on adaptation, organisational learning and knowledge creation. He coaches senior management teams in the 'complexity perspective' and is the creator of PossibilitySpace, a design methodology for enabling creativity and collaboration in groups.

His earlier career in community development and playwork enables him to make an original contribution to groups seeking sustainable change.

He is a frequent speaker at national and international conferences on complexity, organisational learning and knowledge creation and is a visiting lecturer and research associate at Aston Business School, Warwick University, and the Poon Kam Kai Institute of Management, Hong Kong.

Email Arthur Battram at: navcom@mail.com

The Patterns of Organisation

"Contrary to our deepest intuitions, massively disordered systems can spontaneously 'crystallise' a very high degree of order."

Stuart Kauffman

Kauffman's famous phrase 'order for free' describes this process of 'crystallisation', also known as the emergence of complexity in complex adaptive systems. He is telling us not to be surprised by the emergence of order from chaos: the real mystery is how anything simple can ever occur, when all around us, in both the natural world and human culture, we see nothing but complexity and chaos.

The Patterns of Organisation

The 'patterns of organisation' refer to the shape of events and the processes that create, maintain and change them, rather than the structures of buildings or personnel charts. 'Organisation' as a verb, not a noun. In this section, several key ideas are introduced which underpin much of the rest of this book: the nature of systems, the effects of complexity, the crucial insights we can gain from studying complex adaptive systems and a new view of two old ideas, the hierarchy and the network.

Systems

Systems have systems within them. We need to be clear about the relationships between the parts of the system and the whole 'system-in-focus'. All systems are 'perceived systems', dependent on the observer's viewpoint.

Complexity

Because complex systems have built-in unpredictability, the certainties of the 'command and control' approach to management no longer hold true. The implications of complexity theory for organisations are massive.

Complex adaptive systems

Organisations are not machines: try thinking of them as complex adaptive systems. Creative and adaptive behaviour emerges as the agents in a system interact independently.

Network and hierarchy

We need a more complex understanding of the inter-relationships and interdependencies in networks and hierarchies. Networks need hierarchies and hierarchies need networks, and it is crucial to get the relationships right.

Systems

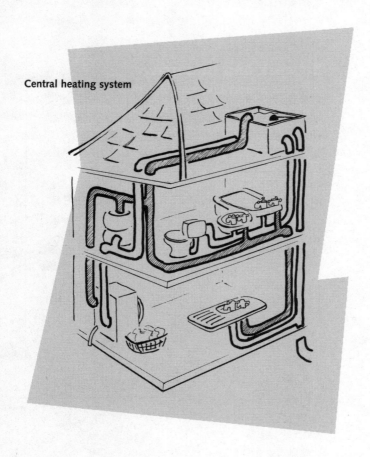

Central heating system

 Relevance

Systems have systems within them. We need to be clear about the relationships between the parts of the system and the whole 'system-in-focus'. All systems are 'perceived systems', dependent on the observer's viewpoint.

Translation

What is a system?

According to Peter Senge, a system is a "perceived whole whose elements 'hang together' because they continually affect each other over time and operate toward a common purpose."

The internal mail service in a company is an example of a system made up of a chain of activities and a network of relationships. The 'mailroom' often has its own staff, but it also works with other administrative staff to make sure that mail reaches the right people.

complex adaptive systems

Emergent wholes and parts

The majority of systems are 'wholes made up of smaller parts which link together' (or 'hang together'). Every system has a separate existence with a name which describes its common characteristics, relationships or functions. For example, a cat, a herd of sheep or a hive of bees are all systems. The parts of a cat such as the liver, or the circulatory system, or the eyes, can also be seen as separate systems of linked components, in the same way the circulatory system contains the heart, the lungs, the arteries and veins: all the parts interrelate to form a functioning whole. Similarly, the individual bees or sheep are parts of the whole hive or herd. Out of this pattern of interrelationships emerges the behaviour of the system, behaviour which is often strikingly different from the behaviour of an individual part. For example, a lone sheep may stand its ground as a person approaches it, but a flock is more likely to edge away. We can see this difference in organisations as well: the creativity of individual staff is often buried in bureaucratic procedures; equally, in an improvising jazz group, the 'feel' and 'flow' of a piece emerges from the pattern of interactions between the players.

Defining a system by its boundary: system-in-focus
Stafford Beer's idea of the 'system-in-focus' is that at any one time you are looking at a sub-system within a larger set of systems. So when we use the phrase 'perceived whole', it implies a necessary degree of subjectivity. For example, it is a matter of opinion whether or not a home-based worker, wholly employed by a company, is part of that organisation or not. On the one hand, the company may be held responsible for the health and safety of its home workers, so in this respect he or she is seen as part of the the company's system. On the other hand, the company may not extend access to job-related benefits such as holidays or sick pay to the

Systems in systems

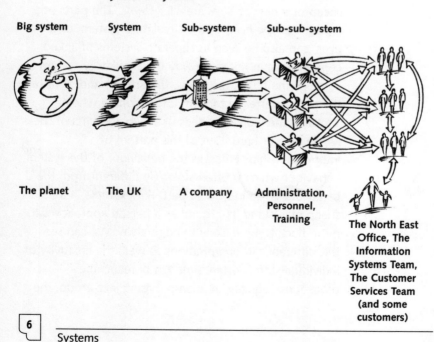

Big system   System   Sub-system   Sub-sub-system

The planet   The UK   A company   Administration, Personnel, Training   The North East Office, The Information Systems Team, The Customer Services Team (and some customers)

homeworker, even if they are paid the same as internal workers. So, in this respect, the homeworker is not a part of the system.

complex adaptive systems

This sort of interaction is part of the behaviour of complex adaptive systems. So in systems thinking, it is important to clearly define the 'system-in-focus'.

What is the system-in-focus?

The problem is that things are never that simple. For example, the North East Office Customer Service Team may include part of the Information Systems Team. And to make matters worse, the Information Systems division may be organised differently, e.g. into only two areas nationally as opposed to ten sales regions. How do we work with our colleagues in Sales when we decide to subdivide Information Systems into smaller units?

System boundaries overlap

As the system-in-focus gets more complex, it brings with it an increase in information (or, more accurately, data). The flood of data starts to overload the processes and systems set up to deal with it. In the past, methods which sought to reduce complexity have had some effect, but the pace of change demands that we now engage with complexity – a process of absorbing it, 'taking it on board', in order to deal with it.

autopoiesis, complexity: reduction vs. absorption

It is the very complexity of complicated systems that has led complexity theorists to develop new approaches to systems which are not based on simplistic mechanical models. As Francisco Varela says:

"Forget the idea of a black box with inputs and outputs. Think in terms of loops."

 ## Application

Everything is a system

When different people, with different interests, link things together in order to describe them, they create a perceived system. This may be taking place within a single organisation or in a partnership involving several organisations. The system can have very different patterns, relationships and intentions depending on the viewpoint of the creator(s). When thinking about change, or implementing change, which of necessity involves other people, it is crucial to establish consensus about:

• the connections: relationships between parts
• a common perspective
• feedback: where and how information about what happens is fed back into the system
• the system-in-focus
• the system boundary.

Systems thinking and its practical applications are explored in detail in *The Fifth Discipline Fieldbook* by Peter Senge and others.

Senge's approach is not a purely traditional systems approach: it incorporates aspects of contemporary ideas such as chaos and complexity theory.

'Meals-on-wheels': what is the system?

Local government in the UK provides a cooked meal delivery service to 'elderly housebound' persons. The 'meals-on-wheels' service, as it is known, purchases food in bulk and produces complete meals in central kitchens. The meals are chilled and transported to local kitchens where they are re-heated and delivered by van or car to the homes of customers.

The management decided to review the system. One persistent problem was 'lumpy gravy'. They examined the whole system and could find nothing wrong. But what is the whole system? The perception of what is or isn't in the system varies with the observer: an elderly person will include their friends and relatives in their view of the system; their social worker may also include their local doctor; the van driver may have heard all about the daughter, but may not know about the friends.

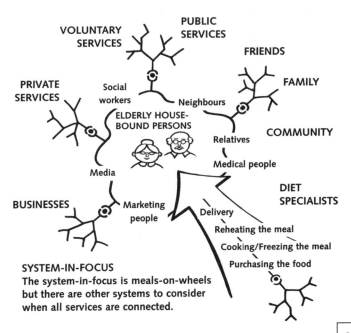

VOLUNTARY SERVICES

PUBLIC SERVICES

FRIENDS

PRIVATE SERVICES

Social workers

FAMILY

Neighbours

ELDERLY HOUSE-BOUND PERSONS

COMMUNITY

Relatives

Media

Medical people

DIET SPECIALISTS

BUSINESSES

Marketing people

Delivery

Reheating the meal

Cooking/Freezing the meal

Purchasing the food

SYSTEM-IN-FOCUS
The system-in-focus is meals-on-wheels but there are other systems to consider when all services are connected.

Discussions about improvements to the system will be very difficult to manage if we are not aware of these differing viewpoints. Why is the gravy lumpy? Is it because of the way it is cooked? Or is it a fault in the chilling? Could it be the reheating? Could it be the driver's fault for delivering it late? If it turns out that the gravy is lumpy because the old lady keeps the meal until teatime, because her daughter cooks for her that day, can we reasonably blame the customer? If we persist in seeing systems as linear delivery chains, then that's about all we can do. Only by viewing the issue as just one small part of the 'whole system', can we start to work together with all the stakeholders to find a solution.

 ## Cross-references
complex adaptive systems, complexity, network and hierarchy, ecosystem, perspectives

 ## References

Stafford Beer, *Diagnosing the System*, John Wiley, 1991, ISBN 0 471 90675 1

John Brockman, *The Third Culture*, Simon & Schuster, 1995, ISBN 0 684 80359 3

Ruth Carter et al, *Systems, Management and Change*, Open University, 1988, ISBN 1 85396 059 4

Humberto Maturana and Francisco Varela, *The Tree of Knowledge: the Biological Roots of Human Understanding*, Shambhala Publications, 1987, ISBN 0 87773 642 1

Peter Senge *et al*, *The Fifth Discipline Fieldbook*, Nicholas Brealey, 1994, ISBN 1 85788 060 9

Complexity

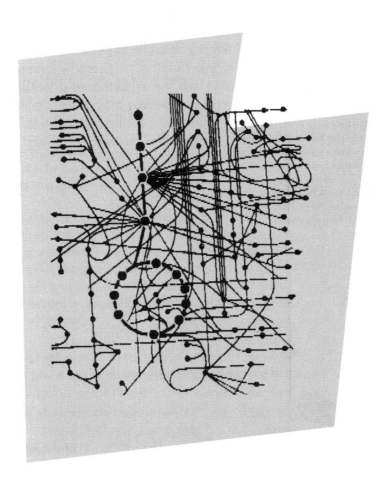

 Relevance

Because complex systems have built-in unpredictability, the certainties of the 'command and control' approach to management no longer hold true. The implications of complexity theory for organisations are massive.

Translation
What is complexity?

The original Greek roots of the word suggest 'entwined together' as in a piece of woven cloth. In everyday speech complexity is a synonym for 'complicatedness': something with many parts and interconnections, and this is also a reasonable summary of its scientific meaning. What makes something complex is not just the variety or number of its components, but their interconnectedness. Although there is no **universally accepted** definition of complexity, the following definition is offered by the Santa Fé Group:

In their book *The Collapse of Chaos*, Jack Cohen and Ian Stewart offer us an insight into complexity by comparing bees and cars. Eggs grow up into bees which lay eggs which grow into new bees. Cohen and Stewart ask us to think about "car factories that make cars that grow into new car factories: that's complexity!"

"Complexity refers to the condition of the universe which is integrated and yet too rich and varied for us to understand in simple common mechanistic or linear ways. We can understand many parts of the universe in these ways but the larger and more intricately related phenomena can only be understood by principles and patterns – not in detail. Complexity deals with the nature of emergence, innovation, learning and adaptation."

Santa Fé Group, 1996

The Santa Fé Group is a group of complexity theorists and management experts linked to the Santa Fé Institute (SFI). The SFI is the world centre for complexity research.

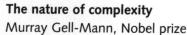

The nature of complexity

Murray Gell-Mann, Nobel prize winner and one of the founders of the Santa Fé Institute, says:

"One of the most important characteristics of complex non-linear systems is that they cannot, in general, be successfully analysed by determining in advance a set of properties or

aspects that are studied separately and then combining those partial approaches in an attempt to form a picture of the whole. Instead, it is necessary to look at the whole system, even if that means taking a crude look, and then allowing possible simplifications to emerge from the work."

Murray Gell-Mann

Because unpredictability is also a characteristic of complex systems, and because scientific definitions focus on predictability, it is difficult to define complexity in traditional scientific terms:

"Instead of relying on the Newtonian metaphor of clockwork predictability, complexity seems to be based on metaphors more akin to the growth of a plant from a tiny seed ... something organic, adaptive, surprising and alive."

Mitchell Waldrop

Two perspectives
In order to understand complexity science we need to look at the roots of 'traditional' science. The Western scientific approach started around about 500-600 BC with **Democritus** who invented early theories of the atom. This 'rational' philosophy was further developed by Descartes in his idea of the duality of mind and body. All science today is therefore an extension of Greek thinking. The basis of the Greek approach was the view that 'there are fixed things which change from time to time'. This view won out over the opposing view, championed by **Heraclitus**, which is summed up by Fritz Perls saying "you can't step into the same river twice": everything is changing all the time in a process of 'becoming'. This view resonates with the idea of 'emergence' in complex adaptive systems, with our ideas about living systems, and with Eastern approaches to philosophy.

perspectives

autopoiesis

Do we understand the world by discovering 'things' or do we invent it?

Do we understand the world by first discovering 'things out there' or do we invent it in our heads? Autopoiesis tells us that we do not perceive the world directly, instead incoming data is filtered by our mental model of the world. Schrödinger, in talking about the effect of the observer in his experiments in quantum mechanics, points to the view commonly held by scientists that they 'stand outside' of their experiments as 'privileged observers', saying 'I'm not needed for all this to happen'. This is the same mistake that managers make pretending that they are outside of the interactions in their teams or departments. The arrogance of the 'privileged observer' idea damages science and because management derives many of its ideas from science, it also damages management.

Complexity: a science that can now emerge

Science uses Plato's approach of 'constructing a likely story'. Until recently, it has not been possible to construct 'likely stories' about complex systems: the computing power needed to construct models of sufficient complexity has not been available. The real revolution can now take place because computers are allowing theorists to study complexity in a scientifically rigorous manner. Computers can run many iterations of scenarios and simulations which produce data which is just as solid as that produced by traditional experimental methods. Twenty years ago when eminent physicists Fritjof Capra and David Bohm wanted to adopt a similar approach without the benefits of computers, they were squeezed out by the scientific establishment.

Keep it synthetic, stupid

In traditional science, if you can predict and control the behaviour of a system you have defined it and therefore you have understood and explained it. This can't be done with living things, nor can it be done with the economy or the weather: all of which are complex systems. Instead, complexity science uses simulation: an approach which can be defined as **synthetic**, because it is about **creating** rather than **analysing** (as in the traditional analytic approach). This lack of traditional prediction and control is not a crucial concern, because in practice we can get a sufficient 'handle' on complexity and complex systems to enable us to use the concepts in a practical way.

As Michael McMaster says:

> *"My (somewhat realised) hope for complexity is that it provides ways of understanding things that do not require any great brain power. It is dependent on patterns and simplification. Complexity, as I understand it, is about making things simpler through patterns (or, as some like to say, compression). My objection to systems dynamics (as I've seen its attempted introduction into a corporate environment) is that it requires too much detail to be dealt with."*

Keep it simulated, scientist

Complexity theorists deal with the problem of prediction and control by using modelling and computer simulation extensively. Kenneth McLeish, in *The Bloomsbury Guide to Human Thought*, describes a computer simulation of basic ant behaviour which illustrates the power of this approach. In the simulation, the ants made an arrangement of eggs in the nest in which the eggs were packed in concentric circles with the largest eggs on the outside of the pile and the smallest on the inside. When this model was tested against observations of real ants, the real ants did exactly the same.

The sciences of complexity

Complexity is not one body of theory: it is a collection of often disparate fields of study which are linked by a common interest in a set of concepts which are not yet perfectly defined.

Complexity sciences include:

- Artificial intelligence
- Cognitive science
- Ecology
- Evolution
- Game theory
- Linguistics
- Social science
- Artificial life
- Computer science
- Economics
- Genetics
- Immunology
- Philosophy.

Unlike traditional science, which studies 'ideal' phenomena, complexity theory studies the phenomena most common in the real world: turbulence and disequilibrium, self-organisation, adaptation, system learning, increasing returns and persistence. These are some of the 'emergent behaviours' which crop up again and again in biological, technological, computational, and economic systems.

Stuart Kauffman relates complexity science to traditional science as follows:

The development of science

Eighteenth century	Newtonian revolution	Developing the sciences of organised simplicity
Nineteenth century	Statistical mechanics	Focusing on disorganised complexity
Twentieth century	Rebirth of biology	Confronting the sciences of organised complexity

adapted from *The Origins of Order*, Kauffman, 1993

Describing complexity – the long and short of it

Gell-Mann looks at complexity in terms of information (the amount of data needed to describe something that is complex) and offers a useful distinction between crude and effective complexity, which will help to throw some light on the question of complexity.

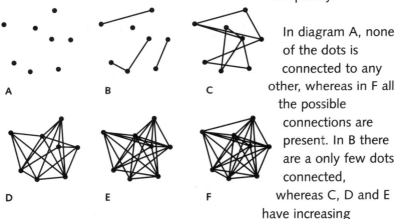

A B C

D E F

In diagram A, none of the dots is connected to any other, whereas in F all the possible connections are present. In B there are a only few dots connected, whereas C, D and E have increasing numbers of connections. But there are other important differences. Gell-Mann explains that B is the 'mirror' image of E in that connections in B are absent in E and vice versa. This is also the case with C and D.

Gell-Mann asks, 'Which pattern is the most complex?' He argues that A and F are not complex because they are easy to describe: A = eight unconnected dots, F = eight totally connected dots. Whereas C and D are very difficult to describe: all the dots would need to be labelled or numbered and then some classification would have to be created to describe the interconnections between them. And what about the 'mirror' nature of the pairings B-E and C-D? How can they be described simply? If we had a special word to describe B, it would then be extremely easy to describe E – all we would need to say is 'reverse-B'. In a very real sense, therefore, complexity is in the eye of the beholder, or more precisely in the language of the beholder.

possibility space, dialogue, perspectives

We feel that the four patterns in the middle (B, C, D and E) are high in information because they are hard to describe, therefore they are relatively complex. So Gell-Mann has located the complexity in the diagrams as being in between the two extremes represented by A and F. His conclusion relates strikingly to another key idea, the 'edge of chaos': in complex systems the complexity is found in the middle, at the fuzzy boundary between states.

the 'edge of chaos', ecosystem

Crude complexity

Gell-Mann links crude complexity to 'algorithmic complexity' in computing. Algorithmic complexity is a measure of how long it will take a computer to work out a problem using its procedures (known as algorithms). The longer it takes to compute, the more algorithmically complex the problem is. Unfortunately this leads us to believe that the random hammerings of a chimpanzee at a typewriter are more complex than a Shakespeare sonnet. This is because random messages cannot be 'compressed' (or made smaller) at all by computers, but a story in English can be compressed because certain patterns of words are repeated. The following two 'strings' of characters will illustrate this:

Random and patterned strings

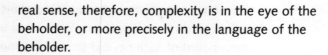

1st string

110110110110110110110110110110110110

111010101000101011110001011010110010

2nd string

The first string is simple: to send it as a message all you need to say is: 'It's the numbers one, one and zero, repeated 12 times'. The second string is algorithmically complex, because it is almost completely random: to send it you would have to list all the numbers; there is no way to compress it.

Effective complexity

Gell-Mann argues that effective complexity is related to the non-random aspects of a system. In the example above, the first string has a small amount of effective complexity because it has regularity (it is a repeating pattern), whereas the second string has no effective complexity and high crude complexity. He argues that effective complexity "can be characterised as the length of a concise description of the regularities of that system or string". So because dot patterns C and D (above) need lengthy descriptions, they are relatively complex; they have comparatively high 'effective complexity'. These dot patterns are also a schematic representation of the 'nodes' and 'connections' in a network; a concept explored extensively by Stuart Kauffman. The number of nodes and the number of connections in a network turn out to have a crucial effect on the behaviour of a system, as can be seen in the table in the next entry (p.29).

network and hierarchy

Application

Operational definition of terms for managers

Michael McMaster has suggested the following as operational definitions for management and organisational purposes:

- chaotic refers to a state where patterns cannot be made or details understood
- complicated refers to a state where patterns cannot

be made but details, parts and sub-systems can be understood

• complex refers to a state where the details cannot be understood but the whole (or general result) can be understood by the ability to make patterns.

Management apes science

The prevailing paradigm of a given era's management theories has historically mimicked the prevailing paradigm of that era's scientific theories. For example, most of science leading up to this century was heavily influenced by the scientific principles of Newton and Descartes. This paradigm tells us that the natural state of a system is equilibrium and that departures from equilibrium will be damped out. Likewise, the approach by which a system was understood was reductionist and deterministic: through understanding the component elements of a system and the manner in which they interact, the future states of the system could (theoretically) be predicted.

Management theory in the nineteenth and early twentieth century also held reductionism, determinism, and equilibrium as core principles – all of social science was influenced by this paradigm. Management theorists such as Fayol and others invented management control mechanisms that are based on the 'organisation as machine' metaphor (Morgan, 1986). Organisational direction is embedded in plans which are then deployed via planning, budgeting, and management-by-objectives systems. A centralised, bureaucratic structure is key in delivering 'command and control' instructions to the workforce. Control is explicit: monetary rewards and punishments are a common form of motivation. Reductionism gave rise to ideas such as division of labour, the idea of task, interchangeability of parts,

Complexity

standard procedures, quality control, cost accounting, time and motion study, and organisational charts. Frederick W. Taylor was responsible for integrating these ideas with the concepts of the scientific method to design a coherent management philosophy. His principles of scientific management have great influence over management practice of today. Taylor believed in a 'social system determinism' – that management of the organisation could be predictable if we understood the science of management. Organisational controls, such as budget, performance review, audits, standards, etc., are used as negative feedback mechanisms for maintaining equilibrium (Wheatley, Margaret, 1994).

The implications of complexity for organisations
The implications of complexity for organisations are massive. Because complex systems have unpredictability built in, the certainties of the 'command and control' approach to management no longer hold true. The bonus with complexity theory is that, unlike chaos theory, there are some powerful suggested steps that organisations can take to move forward in the face of complexity. They are already being implemented with some success by an increasing number of organisations, including US companies Citibank and Xerox. In the UK government sector, the Department of Transport, Devon County Council and Birmingham City Council are busy applying the theories.

Two ways of dealing with complexity
Complexity increases in a system over time; this is a general rule. In the case of living systems, it is known as 'evolution'. Cars get more complicated, computer software gets more complicated. Manufacturers make machines even more complicated by hiding their complexity under a friendly outward appearance: the

familiar controls of a car now hide more computing power than was used to put a man on the moon. Microsoft attempts to make computing easy and fun with Windows. Management theorist Max Boisot describes two ways to deal with complexity: **reduce** it or **absorb** it. Here, it is argued that the former has had its day, and that organisations should focus their efforts on engaging with complexity and absorbing it.

Welcome to the machine: reducing complexity
Ideas derived from control theory and cybernetics (systems dynamics) have influenced organisation theory, and therefore the approach of most large organisations. These approaches treat organisations as if they are machines; seeking to control by reducing variety in the system. There were critics of this approach early on, and it is now unlikely that many organisations would still want to be seen espousing it. As John Darwin explains in *The Wisdom Paradigm*, the problem is that a generally accepted replacement for it has yet to emerge. So, for example, a sales department might communicate to all customers by letter, instead of talking face-to-face to every individual. This reduces complexity but excludes meeting individual needs.

autopoiesis

Resistance to absorbing complexity can be seen as both resistance to change and self-preservation – fundamental characteristics of living systems. Living systems are also complex adaptive systems: which means that they are continually changing and adapting. This apparent paradox is explored further in the entry on 'autopoiesis'.

complex adaptive systems

Increasing complexity
The rise of the customer service idea has meant that this approach to customers has had to be modified greatly: some organisations pride themselves that their approach is now based precisely on meeting individual

system

needs, rather than treating everyone the same. W. Ross Ashby's law of requisite variety warns that "there must be sufficient variety within the controlling system to match that in the system being controlled". In other words, for example, the level of complexity in a sales department must match both the level of complexity in customer need, and the level of complexity in the marketing environment (specialised retail outlets, home selling, mail order, supermarkets, Internet sales etc.) This means that sales departments must, by now, be very complex: they can be considered to be complex adaptive systems. The work of a sales department now involves complex partnerships and contracts with many other organisations. In the past, methods which sought to reduce complexity have had some effect, but the pace of change demands that we now engage more fully with complexity. Management theorist Reg Revans' law of learning states that "the rate of learning must be equal to or greater than the rate of change", which tells us that there needs to be a lot of learning in today's businesses!

Absorbing complexity

metaphor

The pressure for customer service improvements forced many organisations to engage with complexity. When an organisation starts to take on board the immense variety of its interactions with other partners, suppliers and customers, it is absorbing complexity. The old metaphors of control become increasingly inappropriate and begin to constrain the thinking of managers. This is why terminology like networking, partnerships and alliances are increasingly part of the new vocabulary. Alternatives to the machine metaphor are biological metaphors which embody ideas of networking and variety, such as the organism, an ecosystem and the garden. Gardeners know that they

coevolution, ecosystem

cannot fully control their garden; they can only co-control it, sharing it with insects and other wild creatures. They cannot avoid the complexity of the natural world, and if they seek to control it with pesticides and weedkillers the consequences can be expensive and dire, and still the weeds and pests will remain.

The China Syndrome

At the LSE Complexity and Strategy seminar series on 'The Chinese development experience', Professors Max Boisot and John Child gave a paper in which they contrasted Chinese approaches to modernisation and partnership with those of the West. The Chinese, having abandoned their earlier disastrous attempts at planned economy, are now engaged in making the shift from a traditional, often family-based approach, to what Boisot and Child call 'network capitalism'. They argue that Western companies, having developed from fiefs to bureaucracies to markets in the last 250 years, are now also attempting to shift to a network approach. The diagram below is a simplified representation of this process.

The movement towards network capitalism

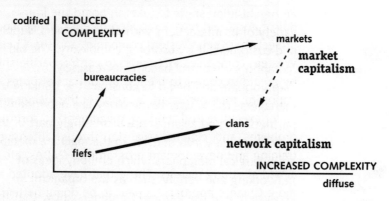

Complexity

The Chinese approach can be seen as absorbing complexity, and the traditional Western approach as reducing complexity. Bureaucracy was developed as a response to the complexity of trade and the Industrial Revolution, later giving way to a market approach, in which freedom of trade is allowed, but in a tightly constrained arena – the market. They argue that the shift to a network approach will be more difficult for the West because it involves absorbing increasing complexity.

The two systems can be compared as follows:

Western	Chinese
Reducing complexity	Absorbing complexity
Formal	Informal
Explicit laws	Implicit laws
Stable, ordered	*Ad hoc*, clannish
Contract rules	Negotiation the norm
Long 'reach'	Limited 'reach'
Ultimately futile attempt to impose the will on the 'landscape' – like 'slash and burn' farming in a forest clearing behind fences	No attempt to change the 'landscape' – small plantings, harvesting wild food, living in the 'landscape'
Short term	Long term

Boisot and Child have examined recent partnership projects between Western companies and the Chinese. Western companies attempted to control partnerships by greater recourse to the law in contract disputes, importing their own staff, bringing in the 'heavy guns' (chief executive and senior management) to sort out problems, and 'cloning' local staff through intensive training and development programmes (MBAs, etc.) aimed at young recruits. Those that have adopted a more Chinese approach appear to be doing better.

Cross-references
network and hierarchy, the 'edge of chaos',
perspectives, autopoiesis, complex adaptive systems

 References

Max Boisot, *Information Space: a Framework for
Learning in Organisations, Institutions and Culture*,
Routledge, 1995, ISBN 0 415 11490 X

Jack Cohen and Ian Stewart, *The Collapse of Chaos:
Discovering Simplicity in a Complex World*, Penguin,
1995, ISBN 0 14 0178740

John Darwin, *The Wisdom Paradigm*, Sheffield
Business School, unpublished paper, 1995

Murray Gell-Mann, *The Quark and the Jaguar:
Adventures in the Simple and the Complex*, Abacus,
1995, ISBN 0 349 10649 5

Stuart Kauffman, *At Home in the Universe*, Oxford
University Press, 1995, ISBN 0 19 509599 5

Stuart Kauffman, *The Origins of Order*, Oxford
University Press, 1993, ISBN 0 19 507951 5

*Kevin Kelly, *Out of Control: the New Biology of
Machines*, Fourth Estate, 1994, ISBN 1 85702 308 0

Kelly describes, often in thriller style, the nature of the huge
changes that complexity-related developments may produce in the
near future. The cover claims that it 'shatters more paradigms per
page than any other book this decade', and certainly the depth and
range of the book is impressive.

*Roger Lewin, *Complexity: Life at the Edge of Chaos*, Macmillan, 1992, ISBN 0 02 570485 0

Lewin's thoughtful best-seller takes in a wider range than the 'other complexity book' by Waldrop (see below), including biologist Brian Goodwin, Gaia theorist James Lovelock and evolutionist critic and zoologist Stephen Jay Gould, in addition to the Santa Fé crowd.

Michael R. Lissack, *Chaos and Complexity: What does that have to do with Management?*, unpublished 1996 paper available at his website: lissack.com/writings

Kenneth McLeish, in *The Bloomsbury Guide to Human Thought*, Bloomsbury Publishing, 1995, ISBN 0 7475 0991 3

Michael McMaster, *The Intelligence Advantage: Organising for Complexity*, Butterworth-Heinemann, 1996, ISBN 0 7506 9792 X

Gareth Morgan, *Images of Organisation*, Sage, 1986, ISBN 0 80392 831 9

Alex Trisioglio, *Managing Complexity*, unpublished paper, London School of Economics, 1995

*M. Mitchell Waldrop, *Complexity: the Emerging Science at the Edge of Order and Chaos*, Penguin, 1994, ISBN 0140179 682

Waldrop's easy-to-read bestseller describes complexity theory in its many guises. It describes the work of the Santa Fé Institute and the personalities involved in creating the 'emerging sciences of complexity'.

*Margaret Wheatley, *Leadership and the New Science*, Berrett-Koehler, 1994, ISBN 1 881052 44 3

*Recommended introductory books

Complex adaptive systems

The octopus: reaching out into its environment

 Relevance

Organisations are not machines: try thinking of them as complex adaptive systems. Creative and adaptive behaviour emerges as the agents in a system interact independently.

Translation

What is a complex adaptive system?

A glib reply is that it is a complex system which can adapt: but what is a complex system? To explain a complex adaptive system, we need to look at both simple and complex systems and their differences. This table sets out the main differences from the complexity standpoint, and these are then explored below.

Simple and complex systems

	Simple system	Chaos: systems which are crudely complex	Complex adaptive system
Number of states	Few possible states	More possible states	A huge number of possible states
Connectivity	Connections between components are fixed	Components are dispersed and completely free to interact locally	Components ('agents') are dispersed and free to interact locally within an hierarchical structure
Behaviour	Simple behaviour – predictable	Disorganised (chaotic) behaviour – largely unpredictable	Emergent behaviour with pockets of unpredictability
Examples	A central heating system or a television set	The weather or a dripping tap; a sand pile that suddenly collapses as more sand is added [like the sand pile in an egg-timer]	All living things, large organisations, ecologies, cultures, politics
Computational state	I and II	III	IV

complexity

The degree of complexity increases down the table, with the number of kinds of interactions (states) and the number of connections increasing the complexity of the system. Some of the terms have special meanings:

- 'local': interactions that take place between neighbouring components, like someone jostling someone else in a queue for a bus
- 'agents': differ from components in that they determine their own behaviour, so birds in a flock, humans in a crowd, or players on

the stock markets are 'agents' whereas water molecules or transistors in a TV are just components

- 'states': a boiler can only be on or off, it is an oscillating system with only two states, so it can transmit a small amount of information, literally one 'bit'. The number of possible states that a human can be in is almost limitless; for example, the same piece of news may make someone happy or sad, or angry. Also the amount of information which can be transmitted is massive
- computational state: explained in the entry 'The edge of chaos'
- connectivity: see 'network and hierarchy'.

the 'edge of chaos', network and hierarchy

complexity

Simple systems

Not all systems are **complex**, some are just **complicated**. A television is a very complicated system – if you look inside you will see lots and lots of tiny parts – but it is not a complex system. The parts all connect in simple, pre-determined ways. A

system

central heating system is also a simple system in which a few parts, connected in a specific way, carry out a predetermined task: the thermostat detects a fall in room temperature and signals to the boiler, which pumps hot water to the radiators which raise the room temperature until the thermostat detects that the temperature is now at the programmed level and so signals the boiler to turn off. This circular activity, which restricts the boiler, is known as a negative feedback loop. Inputs and outputs are

increasing returns and lock-in

determined; the number of states is two (heat on or heat off; temperature high enough or too low). The system's behaviour is completely predictable.

Chaos: complex systems

self-organisation

Chaotic systems such as the weather are non-linear systems which show 'sensitivity to initial conditions'. This is popularly known as the 'butterfly effect', described by the meteorologist Edward Lorenz as "a butterfly flapping its wings over the Amazon leads

Complex adaptive systems

to a hurricane on the other side of the world".

A non-linear effect doesn't vary smoothly with input: the outcome is unpredictable and can vary wildly; unlike a linear effect in which a small change in the input to a system leads to a small change in the output. All complex systems are unpredictable, and what **can** be predicted is very constrained. With the weather, unpredictability increases with time and detail: you can predict the weather outside your office five minutes from now with some confidence, and you can guess the overall temperature in December in your region, but you cannot predict the weather in Tokyo in nine months time. The behaviour of the economy, like the weather, is also splendidly non-linear, as Black Wednesday demonstrated (although the economy is not just a chaotic system; it is a complex adaptive system which includes some unpredictability).

Chaotic sandpiles: self-organised criticality
The sandpile metaphor is an example of 'self-organised criticality': a term current in chaos theory, first used by Per Bak. When a pile of sand has more sand added to it in some way, there comes a point when the pile suddenly collapses. In the egg timer, the sand is steadily dribbled down onto the pile; in a huge dune in the Sahara it is the action of wind removing sand from one dune and depositing it on another that causes the collapse. The method makes no difference to the concept. The sandpile is 'self-organised' because it reaches this critical state without any outside agency.

The point is this: for any given sandpile there is a point at which this collapse becomes very likely to happen: not will it collapse, but when? This is the point of 'criticality'. In chaos language, it is a bifurcation point – the graph suddenly bifurcates (splits into two states) leaving a smaller pile and some loose sand sliding down the sides. Try as you might, it won't get any higher. It's a sort of diminishing return; the system locks in to that size of pile. This criticality can be seen in many natural systems: in solar activity, in water currents and earthquakes; it is an example of a phase transition.

increasing returns and lock-in

the 'edge of chaos'

The ideas of chaos theory generated a lot of media interest in the late 80s, and many management theorists rushed to apply it, with disappointing results. Chaos is now considered to be a subset of complexity theory, which is also being applied to organisations rather more successfully.

Complex adaptive systems: 'order for free'
A further important distinction is that between a 'complex system' and a 'complex **adaptive** system': the weather is a complex system, but an organisation or an ant colony are examples of complex adaptive systems, because they are not just **complex**, they also **adapt** to their environment. A chaotic system like a pile of sand has little or no internal structure, the interactions between the components are local only and they exhibit a degree of unpredictability. A complex adaptive system, however, is both self-organising and learning; other examples include social systems, economies, cultures, and political systems.

Complex adaptive systems

network and hierarchy, fitness landscape

In a complex adaptive system, the components are not totally 'free': they are constrained by certain linkages to each other, and there is a higher level of structure, often of a hierarchical nature. The result can often be the emergence of new predictable behaviour – what Stuart Kauffman describes as 'order for free'.

Emergence

In systems such as the economy, the actions of individual players in the market are not co-ordinated in any way, yet the overall behaviour of the market emerges from the combined impact of their actions. Also, the interchanges among the components of a complex adaptive system can cause significant changes in the nature of the components themselves, and have important consequences for the system as a whole. These interactions are non-linear; there is a range of possible responses each component or agent can make, depending on its circumstances, so a certain level of unpredictability of response exists. It is as if everyone in a company can constantly re-negotiate their own job description at the same time as they constantly reorganise their work, and improve the way they deliver it!

self-organisation

All complex adaptive systems model their environment

autopoiesis

A complex adaptive system appears to be 'adaptively intelligent' – constantly seeing and imagining patterns, testing ideas, acting upon them, discarding them again – always evolving and learning. This applies to a bacterium as well as a human. A bacterium 'knows' that an increasing concentration of a food chemical means that food is nearby: the bacterium has 'modelled' its environment in exactly the same way that a human being does. Murray Gell-Mann, describing commonalities between learning and thinking in animals and human beings and the evolution of societies, says that:

> "... the common feature of all these processes is that in each one a complex adaptive system acquires information about its environment and its own interaction with that environment, identifying regularities in that information, condensing those regularities into a kind of 'schema' or model, and acting in the real world on the basis of that schema. In each case, there are various competing schemata, and the results of the action in the real world feed back to influence the competition among those schemata."

Levels of organisation and interaction

Unlike bacteria, most complex adaptive systems have many levels of organisation, with agents at any one level serving as the building blocks for agents at a higher level. For example:

John Holland (quoted by Waldrop) says that there is no such thing as a solitary complex adaptive system, because all complex adaptive systems are parts of other complex adaptive systems. So, in fact, complex adaptive systems only come into being within already existing complex adaptive systems, like organisms within an ecosystem for example. Holland's statement is reminiscent of Stafford Beer's idea of the 'system-in-focus': at any one time, you are looking at a sub-system within a larger set of systems. But we must not forget that these systems are not fixed entities; they are dependent on our point of view.

system, perspectives

Complex adaptive systems are constantly revising and rearranging their components in response to feedback from the environment. Examples are to be found in the evolution of organisms, the brain changing connections between neurons, firms reshuffling their departmental structure, countries realigning their alliances. At some deep, fundamental level, all these processes of learning, evolution and adaptation are the same. And one of the fundamental mechanisms of adaptation in any given system is this revision and recombination of the building blocks.

network and hierarchy, fitness landscape

Complex adaptive systems typically have many niches, each one of which can be exploited by an agent adapted to fill that niche. New opportunities are always being created by the system. It is therefore essentially meaningless to talk about a complex adaptive system being 'in equilibrium': the system can never achieve balance. It is always moving on. Let's be clear: if a complex adaptive system ever does reach equilibrium, it isn't just stable, it's dead. Agents in the system can never 'optimise' their 'fitness' or their utility. The space of possibilities is too vast; they have no practical way of finding the optimum. The most they can ever do is to change and improve themselves relative to what the other agents are doing. In short, a complex adaptive system is characterised by perpetual novelty. Kauffman and others have proposed that organisms increase the complexity of their interactions with others in such a way that they reach the boundary between order and randomness (the 'edge of chaos'), thereby maximising the average fitness of the organisms.

the 'edge of chaos'

"It turns out that in a wide variety of coupled systems the highest mean fitness is at the phase transition between order and chaos."

Stuart Kauffman

Note 1: Portions of the above material are adapted from John Darwin's unpublished paper 'The Wisdom Paradigm', used with thanks.

Note 2 on terminology: 'Complex adaptive system' is the term preferred by the Santa Fé Institute (SFI). The LSE complexity research programme has proposed the alternative 'complex evolving system' to refer to human complex adaptive systems. Their view is that human systems are theoretically different from other systems in that they can learn and change their internal structure. Both these characteristics are present, however, in natural systems such as ant colonies and primate groups. It is also by no means clear that the term 'evolving' can be applied to human systems: some commentators would argue that by definition human systems are 'outside' evolution. For these reasons (and others not noted here), the SFI term is therefore preferred.

Two views of complex adaptive systems: 'pushing out' and 'pulling in'

The 'outward urge' of the complex adaptive system results from the independent agents or sub-systems within the complex adaptive system, each seeking to improve their situation. This is represented by the 'pushing out' of the arrows in the illustration below left. This is contrasted with the diagram on the right,

Complex adaptive systems

representing autopoiesis – the self-preserving tendency of all organisms – as an 'inward urge' to retreat to the core of the identity; the 'me' as opposed to everything out there that is 'not me'. The shape is intended to be reminiscent of an amoeba retracting itself inwards (the arrows indicating this 'pulling in'). It is characteristic of a system as an individual entity, preserving itself. Here we represent the complex adaptive system as an octopus and autopoiesis as a hedgehog.

The complex adaptive system

The autopoietic system

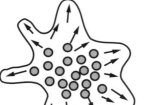

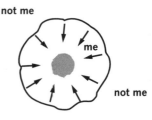

not me

me

not me

autopoiesis

The difference is about focus. When the focus is on the system as a single entity, we need to be aware of autopoeisis; when we focus on a system as a complex adaptive system we need to be aware of the interactions of the individual elements of the system which give rise to emergent behaviour. This emergence is shown in the diagram below:

Emergence in complex adaptive systems

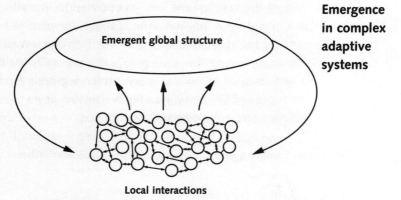

Emergent global structure

Local interactions

A global structure emerges from the local interactions of individual agents, which feeds back to influence the behaviour of the individuals.

Application
The enterprising amoeba

metaphor

self-organising, network and hierarchy, ecosystem, the 'edge of chaos'

Complex adaptive systems are a powerful metaphor offering insights into the underlying processes in the life of organisations. Peter Fryer, Managing Director of a UK Training and Enterprise Council (TEC), sees his organisation as constantly striving to improve its 'fit' to its environment, like an organism in an ecosystem. After spending many years as a management trainer in the civil service, and with a background in nuclear physics, he now uses leading-edge complexity science to help him manage 150 people whom he encourages to act as independent agents in a series of self-organising networks. He trusts that emergence will take place and it does: the TEC is highly regarded both by its political masters and the local community for its responsiveness and commitment to 'releasing potential'. He describes the TEC as an 'amoeba':

Complex adaptive systems

able to react quickly because the restrictive internal scaffolding of organisation charts and management hierarchy have been removed from within it. Networking is at the core of everyone's work and the principles of self-organisation are used to drive teamworking. When you want people to work in the zone of possibility at the 'edge of chaos' you need to support them appropriately: these risky sounding processes are underpinned by a constantly re-evaluated corporate culture based on a set of shared values developed with the involvement of all staff from every level of the organisation.

 ## Cross-references
the 'edge of chaos', system, autopoiesis, network and hierarchy, fitness landscape, perspectives

 ## References

John Darwin, *The Wisdom Paradigm*, Sheffield Business School, unpublished paper, 1995

Murray Gell-Mann, *The Quark and the Jaguar: Adventures in the Simple and the Complex*, Abacus, 1995, ISBN 0 349 10649 5

James Gleick, *Chaos: Making a New Science*, Abacus, 1988, ISBN 0 349 10525 1

Stuart Kauffman, *At Home in the Universe*, Oxford University Press, 1995, ISBN 0 19 509599 5

Roger Lewin, *Complexity: Life at the Edge of Chaos*, Macmillan, 1992, ISBN 0 02 570485 0

Network and
hierarchy

Relevance

We need a more complex understanding of the inter-relationships and interdependencies in networks and hierarchies. Networks need hierarchies and hierarchies need networks, and it is crucial to get the relationships right.

Translation

Just do it

The building's on fire. What do we do? Call a meeting? Of course not, we get out as fast as we can and call the fire brigade. Do they call a meeting? Of course not; they leap into action as a highly skilled unit with one person in charge. You don't want a network standing around outside a raging fire trying to come to a consensus on approaches to the problem.

Mind you...

> "At IBM, the emergent expert was a surprise to everyone, including the expert himself. Neither he, nor his manager, realised how 'central' he was in disseminating and compiling information on a new strategic technology."
>
> Valdis Krebs, a US consultant specialising in network ideas, in a posting to the Learning Organisation email discussion group

Hierarchy or network?

It is possible to read the complexity science in this book as a sustained attack on the idea of hierarchy. Self-organisation – in which individual agents form 'flocks', with no leader; learning without any central controller; natural selection in which random genetic changes produce steady improvements in life on earth – all seem to be saying that hierarchy has no place in the world. Applied to organisations, the message appears to be 'destroy the hierarchy', 'let people determine their own networks', and 'a better organisation will emerge from the chaos'.

That is not the message here. Networks need hierarchies and hierarchies need networks, and it is crucial to get the relationships right. Get hierarchy wrong and an oppressive bureaucracy stamps out networking which results in the stifling of innovation and learning. Too much networking and the building burns down around us while we are in a meeting.

Why we need hierarchy

The following story by Herbert Simon, the Nobel Prize-winning economist and theorist of public administration, reminds us of the rationality of the hierarchy. Simon tells the story of two watchmakers: Hora and Tempus. Both make exquisite thousand-piece watches which are in high demand. For both of them the phone doesn't stop ringing, but while Hora prospered, Tempus went bust... why? The two watchmakers used completely different methods. Tempus put his together piece by piece, whereas Hora made little units of ten or so pieces and then put them together to make the complete watch. When the phone rang at Hora's shop he would have to interrupt his work to answer it and the unit he had nearly finished would fall apart. This didn't make a lot of difference to him, but when the phone interrupted Tempus it was a different story: he would lose all the work he had done that morning, putting together hundreds of the separate pieces of his watch. The more his phone rang the more work he lost until his shop went bankrupt.

So the best way to organise a team is to put someone in charge to tell the team members what to do and how to do it? No that's not the message either. Here's why.

Features of Boolean NK networks

Stuart Kauffman, of the Santa Fé Institute, studies what he calls Boolean NK networks: computer simulations of interconnected light-bulbs. The light-bulb network is an extremely simple and general simulation of an NK network and consists of many independent 'agents' or components: the 'agents' interact locally and the emergent behaviour of the system is independent of the internal structure of the components. His reason for first studying these networks was to uncover the control mechanism that determined the switching of genes in the development of organisms. Over the years, his work has developed much broader applications, including looking at enzyme reactions; studying 'autocatalytic sets' of chemicals which may represent the way life itself evolved; and the development of the economy, in collaboration with Brian Arthur – also at the Santa Fé Institute.

In a Boolean NK network, the light-bulbs are wired up to each other in various ways with switches controlling the individual bulbs. N stands for 'node' and K for 'connection', hence NK network; the Boolean part describes the rules for switching, based on statements in 'Boolean logic'. For example: 'if A then B', 'if A and B then C' and so on. In terms of the NK network, 'A and B then C' might mean, 'if light-bulb A is on, and light-bulb B is also on, then light-bulb C should switch on'. If the condition isn't met then C stays unlit. The interactions between the light-bulbs are 'local', i.e there is no top-down organisation, no hierarchy, no central control, just as we see in cellular automata like the 'game of life'.

complex adaptive systems/what is a complex adaptive system?, the 'game of life'

Connectedness

Kauffman was studying the **connectedness** of his networks in order to understand the role of genes in development. We now know that genes exist in networks: each gene is typically controlled by between two and ten other genes: these interactions, amongst other things, determine the number of types of cell in an organism. Kauffman was trying to work out the mathematics of this connectedness. He had estimated that if there were **many** connections in the network the thing would go crazy, flashing lights on and off in a completely random way, because each change would trigger another change right across the network. Equally, with only one connection between each node, the network would be too simple and a static pattern would just blink on and off. (These two extremes are now familiar to complexity science as Class I and III, stasis and chaos.) He built a huge simulation of a hundred genes: the number of possible states in this case is 2^{100} (two multiplied by itself a hundred times, which is about one million trillion trillion, or 1 followed by 30 zeros!).

the 'edge of chaos'

'Order for free'
When the simulation was run he made a surprising discovery: rather than the chaotic flashing light patterns he'd been expecting, the network quickly settled down into relatively few simple states. The result was entirely unexpected. Instead of exploring the 'space' of a million trillion trillion states, the network quickly moved into a tiny corner of the space and stayed there. From the space of all possible combinations, the network quickly selected an ordered yet flexible cycle of states, the number of states in the cycle being roughly related to the square root of the number of genes in the simulated network. When Kauffman researched the comparable data on real organisms, he found that they also obeyed this rule: the number of cell types was roughly equal to the square root of the number of genes in the organism. Since his original discovery, this effect – which Kauffman calls 'order for free' in which a relatively small number of states are preferred out of a huge range of possible states – has been replicated in many other simulations of biological phenomena. For example, it is present in both the 'boids' simulation and the 'game of life'.

self-organisation, the 'game of life'

Network and hierarchy

"By selecting an appropriate strategy, organisms tune their coupling to their environment to whatever value suits them best. And if they adjust the coupling to their own advantage, they will reach the boundary between order and randomness – the regime of peak average fitness. The bold hypothesis is that complex adaptive systems adapt to and thrive on the edge of chaos. [...]It now begins to appear that systems in the complex regime can carry out and co-ordinate the most complex behaviour and adapt most readily and can build the most useful models of their environments."

Stuart Kauffman

Crystallisation of connected webs

Ratio of threads to buttons: 0.25

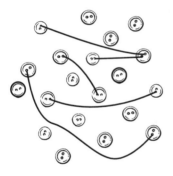

Ratio of threads to buttons: 0.75

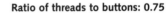

Ratio of threads to buttons: 1.0

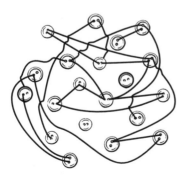

Ratio of threads to buttons: 1.25

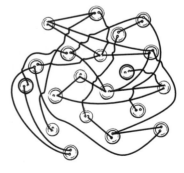

Adapted from *At Home in the Universe*

When a system moves to the 'edge of chaos' it is moving to the point of a 'phase transition'; in this case between order and chaos. Kauffman offers a 'toy problem' to explain how variations in connectedness lead to this 'phase transition'.

Buttons and threads: crystallisation of connected webs
Kauffman asks us to imagine a version of a 'random graph' in which a number of buttons are connected to each other with threads.

Start by scattering 20 buttons on a tabletop. Randomly choose two buttons, connect them with a thread and put them back where they were. Do the same with another two buttons. At first, as you pick up pairs of buttons, you will almost certainly be picking up unconnected buttons. After a while, however, you are much more likely to be picking up buttons that are already connected to other buttons. What is happening is that you are randomly connecting the buttons into clusters. This is shown in the 'crystallisation of connected webs' diagram. Each cluster of buttons is known as a component in the emerging network. When the number of threads is low compared to the number of buttons, there are few connections (known as edges or arcs) and several components. As the ratio of threads to buttons increases towards 1 most of the buttons become connected to each other: this is a phase transition similar to the point at which water freezes into ice. As the ratio increases, a single giant component 'crystallises'. This effect occurs in all sizes of network from the tiny toy problem with only 20 buttons, right up to networks of many thousands of nodes. The phase transition is shown in the diagram opposite:

Network and hierarchy

Crystallisation of connected webs – a phase transition

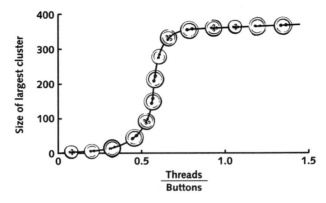

Adapted from *At Home in the Universe*

In this diagram the number of threads ranges from 0 to 600 with the number of buttons fixed at 400.

Don't freeze the network

So we have a general principle of networks: with few connections, the individual elements are isolated and information cannot be transmitted across the network. (In the simulations of light-bulb networks, information is represented by the signals that turn the bulbs on and off.) Too many connections and the network freezes up. These ideas have already been applied to both human and computer networks. Kevin Kelly describes one of the counter-intuitive consequences of what he calls "network logic":

- more roads – less speed. In the 1960s, traffic planners in Stuttgart added an extra street to ease traffic: traffic got **worse**. In 1992, fearing the worst on Earth Day in New York, the City Council closed 42nd street. Traffic congestion went **down**.

A new perspective on network and hierarchy

We need a more complex understanding of the inter-relationships and interdependencies of networks and hierarchies. Where do hierarchy and networks come from? They come from our sense of self: our identity is the common link between them. Autopoiesis tells us that all living systems maintain and recreate their identity, distinguishing between 'me' and 'not me'. We all make this distinction as babies: it is the emergence of hierarchy. Later it is followed by the realisation, known as 'theory of mind' (as described by Robin Dunbar), that other children are also 'people like me', not just objects in the environment. It is at this point that network emerges. We have a choice; we can continue to see others as being in a hierarchy in relation to ourselves or we can acknowledge that we are part of a community, a network. It is the choice between a top-down view in which network is the servant of hierarchy, and a bottom-up view in which the need for hierarchy emerges from the network, and the two are interdependent.

autopoiesis

Management theorists, Lipnack and Stamps, argue that there is a shift going on from a predominantly hierarchical world to one in which hierarchies and networks will coexist and co-evolve.

Complexity theory tells us that complex adaptive systems are constantly revising and rearranging their components in response to feedback from the environment – unmaking and remaking the interconnections between the hierarchies and networks within them.

The hierarchy and the network views of 'me' and 'not me'

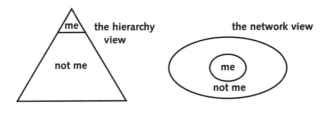

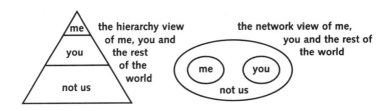

> *"The world will be more networked, but hierarchies will not go away – they just won't dominate the way they have in the past."*
>
> Lipnack and Stamps

 ## Application
Network emergence (and how to kill a network)

Valdis Krebs, a US consultant specialising in network ideas, believes that the application of Kauffman's notion of 'network emergence' to the learning organisation rests in achieving cultures in which different kinds of connectivity between individuals are encouraged, especially in response to the environment of the organisation, whether market or service-oriented. Conversely, if links are removed past a certain point, networks in organisations will simply fall apart. He explains that:

> *"If you examine the connectivity within a community (set), as random links (arcs) are made between individuals (nodes), a striking phenomenon occurs which I refer to as the 'avalanche' (in random graph evolution it is called the 'double jump'). Describing it from the perspective of a growing number of links, what happens is that at a certain point in the link density, the connectivity of the community suddenly skyrockets to include almost everyone (where connectivity includes indirect connections between individuals). At the same time there is a rapid coalescence of various sub-communities which have already formed.*
>
> *The opposite phenomenon occurs with the removal of links from a connected community. Suddenly, its connectivity rapidly disintegrates leaving a dispersed 'archipelago' of relatively small sub-communities."*
>
> Valdis Krebs in a posting to the Learning Organisation
> email discussion group

(These isolated communities can be clearly seen in the 'crystallisation of connected webs' diagram on p.45.)

The clear message here is that careful nurturing of informal networks (which is often as simple as just leaving them alone) can create a benign phase transition under which improvements can rapidly ripple across the organisation. This can be clearly seen in the case of receiver-based communication (a radio-based network communication initiative for mobile repair staff within the Xerox corporation), as can the consequences of interference. The original initiative had been driven by the chief executive, working with a team of management consultants. Some time after the introduction of the walkie-talkie based system had achieved excellent improvements in productivity, middle management tried to abolish it, by taking away the radios. But by this time the system was so well

receiver-based communication (RBC)

embedded, because the benefits were so clear to all the repair workers, that the workers simply went out and bought their own radios! The chief executive intervened and slowly the system came to be valued by the management hierarchy.

Informal networks in knowledge-based organisations
In most departments in large organisations, there are a few key people that most people turn to for information or advice. These individuals are nodes in an informal network, yet they may not even be aware of the pivotal role that they play. (This should not be surprising if we realise that, even in quite densely connected networks, relatively few people are in direct contact with others outside of their own small work area.) Valdis Krebs, of Krebs & Associates, reports research findings that show that no-one was consciously aware of who those informal leaders were – not even the leaders themselves – until researchers investigated and discovered who was performing what leadership function. One quiet, unassuming individual who was nowhere near the top of the organisation chart was discovered to be the person whose opinions most strongly influenced the corporation's priorities. In both of the two cases researched, management resisted the temptation to formalise the informal. They made informal interventions instead, which revolved around including the 'hidden resource' in new networks and teams (some of which were formal 'task forces') to allow others access to their expertise. He reports that this informal 'social engineering' seems to be more effective than re-engineering (as in Business Process Re-engineering [BPR]) in knowledge-based organisations. What is interesting here is that by being well-connected, these informal network 'nodes' gained even more connections – the concept of 'increasing returns' in action.

increasing returns and lock-in

'TeamNets': networking across hierarchies

Many working parties and task groups never acquire an independent status. The need of managers to control process and outcomes means that the benefits of self-organised collaboration for mutual benefit rarely emerge. To meet the need for networking in complex bureaucracies, Jessica Lipnack and Jeffrey Stamps have developed the concept of 'TeamNets'. TeamNets can organise themselves and achieve excellent results operating at the edge of the organisation, without losing control.

The Central Library Management Team of Birmingham City Council in the UK, responsible for the lending library service across the whole city, introduced TeamNets as a way of encouraging voluntary relationships in team formation, information exchange and problem-solving. A mechanism for sharing just enough information between each TeamNet was introduced to prevent overload, while giving the management team enough knowledge about what the TeamNets were doing and achieving. This met the needs of both management and workers. Leadership became shared among the TeamNets as informal relationships developed; the members being driven by mutual interest in achieving a good result for the service. Communication across teams was enhanced by having at least one management team member in the TeamNets. TeamNets clearly embody the principles of optimal connectedness discovered by Kauffman.

How can informal networks become formal parts of the organisation?

Jessica Lipnack feels that there is a prejudice against networks being regarded as 'real' organisations. They are viewed as good for informal processes but they are not seen as the sort of organisation that gets anything concrete done. Lipnack, in collaboration with Jeffrey Stamps, has spent the past 17 years researching and writing about the ways in which networks can become 'organisations for the 21st century' and they have documented several thousand examples in their books.

The processes used most frequently to formalise informal networks that they have observed are:

1. Clarify the purpose (Why are we doing this?)
2. Identify the members (Who is involved?)
3. Establish the links (How are we connected?)
4. Multiply the leaders (Who is responsible for what?)
5. Integrate the levels (How are we connected to the hierarchy and the 'lower-archy'?)

They suggest that having gone through these steps, sophisticated modelling tools should be used to develop clear work plans. They use a package called TeamFlow, which is a cross-functional deployment chart modelling tool that allows you to represent neatly each of the five steps in the work of a network listed above.

They cite many documented successes – from the small business networking miracle that turned Denmark's economy around in the late 1980s, to Eastman Chemicals' extensive use of cross-boundary teams (alias networks) to accomplish all of their work.

Lipnack and Stamps regard networks – both informal and formal ones – as the successors to hierarchy and bureaucracy, not replacements for them but additions to them.

Cross-references
the 'edge of chaos', self-organisation, complex adaptive systems, coevolution, ecosystem

References

Robin Dunbar, *Grooming, Gossip and the Evolution of Language*, Faber, London, 1996, ISBN 0 571 17396 9

Niles Eldredge, *Reinventing Darwin*, Weidenfeld and Nicholson, 1995, ISBN 0 297 81603 9

Stuart Kauffman, *At Home in the Universe*, Oxford University Press, 1995, ISBN 0 19 509599 5

Kevin Kelly, *Out of Control: the New Biology of Machines*, Fourth Estate, 1994, ISBN 1 85702 308 0

Jessica Lipnack and Jeffrey Stamps, *The Age of the Network*, John Wiley, 1994, ISBN 0 471 14740 0

M. Mitchell Waldrop, *Complexity: the Emerging Science at the Edge of Order and Chaos*, Penguin, 1994, ISBN 0140 179 682

Landscapes of
Possibility

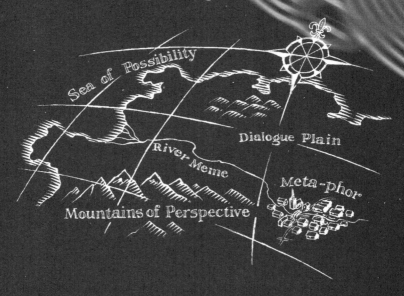

Sea of Possibility

Dialogue Plain

River Meme

Meta-phor

Mountains of Perspective

"Effective searching procedures become, when the search-space is sufficiently large, indistinguishable from true creativity."

Richard Dawkins

'Landscapes of possibility' is another way of describing the search-space to which Dawkins refers. This section focuses on the necessary learning, communication and possibility without which we cannot hope to cope with complexity. Using dialogue and metaphor, we can walk the landscapes of possibility, examining our world from many different perspectives, searching out creative solutions to complex problems.

Landscapes of Possibility

Dialogue
Dialogue is a special kind of conversation. Dialogue is about **emergence**: the bringing forth of new and previously hidden meanings and understandings. Dialogue is the tool by which we can explore possibility space.

Memes
The idea of the meme is an attempt to explain the transmission of human culture. It is important to be aware of the constraints which memes impose on our attempts to create change, because we cannot control them; the best we can hope for is to influence their transmission.

Metaphor
Metaphors help us to link ideas in new ways so that new knowledge can emerge. They are a powerful way of using language to engage with complexity.

Receiver-based communication (RBC)
RBC is a key example of a communication system designed to take advantage of network possibilities.

Perspectives

To engage with complexity, we need perspectives which admit the possibility that more than one thing can be true at once.

Possibility space

When change is constant, creativity and adaptation are crucial. Possibility space can embrace complexity: it is both a search strategy and a design strategy for the creation of possibilities.

Dialogue

possibility space

Relevance

Dialogue is a special kind of conversation. Dialogue is about **emergence**: the bringing forth of new and previously hidden meanings and understandings. Dialogue is the tool by which we can explore possibility space.

Translation

"I'm more intelligent when I talk to you."

Arthur Battram in dialogue during the writing of this book with
Steve Trivett, an organisational learning consultant

*"One of the most interesting things is that larger order
things emerge from the interaction of smaller things. [...]
I think it's possible that the part of our mind that does
information processing is in large part a cultural artefact.
A human who's not brought up around other humans isn't
a very smart machine at all. Part of what makes us smart
is our culture and our interactions with others."*

Danny Hillis, inventor of the 'connection machine', a computer
that imitates evolution to solve problems, quoted in *The Third
Culture*

Listening and thinking

Let's state the obvious: dialogue involves two acts –
talking and listening. Most of us can talk quite well;
some of us may have honed our small talk for use in
tricky moments over the finger buffet; we may even
have gone on training courses in public speaking. It is
far less likely that we have given the same attention to
listening, and if we have at all, it is likely to have been
in a counselling or therapy setting, rather than at
work. Managers don't usually get promoted for
listening to people. Yet as Michael McMaster says:

*"Good therapists, top sales people, effective executives
and managers realise that listening encompasses far more
understanding and far more power than is generally
realised."*

Exploring possibility space

Dialogue is a special kind of conversation. It requires
people to listen and think at the same time, which isn't
easy. As a result, dialogue requires the application of

some simple rules which allows one person to speak unchallenged, while others listen and seek clarification of their understanding (a similar idea is used in Revans' Action Learning method). Supportive questioning (which is really best seen as an extension of listening) is allowed, but challenging the underlying belief system, or value system, is not allowed.

Dialogue is about **emergence:** the bringing forth of new and previously hidden meanings and understandings. (See the three rules for dialogue on p.63.) Dialogue is the tool by which we can explore possibility space.

possibility space

An example: dialogue for access

A UK housing provider created dialogue sessions – or we could say they 'designed a possibility space' – to explore what was blocking certain groups of users from using the services. As a result of the dialogue initiative, they set up special advice sessions for Asian women. By listening to the women telling their own stories within the dialogue sessions (which provided many insights into the low service uptake), it was also possible to 'unpack' the complex relationships, values and belief systems which can generate conflict when not properly understood.

In his book *Grooming, Gossip and the Evolution of Language*, Robin Dunbar describes his theory that language evolved from grooming behaviour in small groups of early humans when, for survival reasons, the size of the group increased such that grooming as 'social glue' was no longer possible. Language then developed as a sort of 'vocal grooming' which then became gossip. Ralph Rosnow, author of a book on the 'social psychology of hearsay', said in an interview in *Psychology Today* that what is often denigrated as 'gossip' actually serves important social and psychological functions as a unifying force to 'hold us all together'. He says that if people aren't talking about other people, it is a signal that something is wrong, that there is some alienation or indifference.

"Language evolved to facilitate bonding through the exchange of social information."

Robin Dunbar

Dialogue is a complex dynamic process which allows alternative solutions to emerge at the same time as problems and issues are surfacing. Often only a few words will be used to point to huge submerged issues. 'Unpacking' in this context refers to the way certain words carry a whole collection of meanings, thoughts, feelings and experiences for the speaker or speakers. To be able to unpack these 'compressed words' we must be able to suspend our assumptions, question the rationale behind existing arrangements, and view dialogue as a way of 'getting closer' to what different groups are trying to communicate to us. If questions are perceived to be supportive and non-threatening, this will help people share their views and feelings.

complex adaptive systems, self-organisation

Dialogue in a group can be likened to a complex adaptive system because emergence will happen only if the initial conditions (rules and relationships) are right; only if the interactions are self-referential and reinforcing; and only if the interactions contain feedback (both positive and negative). If dialogue partners view the process of dialogue simply as the sending and receiving of messages, then the dialogue will almost certainly fail.

"Sending and receiving is a rather old-fashioned and mechanistic view of communication. It's a view that in my experience gets organisations into all kinds of trouble. A dialogue or a conversation occurs in (or emerges from) the interaction of two or more people, and the idea of sender and receiver is neither technically accurate nor, in my opinion, a very powerful interpretation. Nothing is

autopoiesis

*communicated directly to another. All communications go
through interpretations: processes of context, meaning,
significance, content, etc. Even apparently sensible
speaking is frequently merely noise to its intended
recipient."*

Michael McMaster

Application
Dialogue in improvement and change initiatives

In a dialogue group everyone must be given their
chance to explain something from their own
perspective, from which a wide range of previously
unquestioned views and opinions can then be
explored. It is important that everyone is allowed to
express and explain what they mean. This is
fundamental to an understanding of the 'whole
organisation'. Some simple rules, like everyone being
given the same amount of time to talk about their
experiences and feelings without interruption, need to
be employed. This is vital if open and honest
responses are to emerge: a wide variety of ideas must
be absorbed so that conflicting and reinforcing
thoughts can 'self-organise' in people's minds. It is
these simple rules which enable new possibilities to
emerge, knowledge to be extended and assumptions
to be challenged. It works because everyone wants to
feel they are being treated fairly. Individuals are then
able to bring unknown parts of the bigger picture
together at a conscious level. This is why dialogue
rather than discussion generates more possibilities and
more learning.

An example of dialogue rules

These particular rules were used within a number of
problem-solving sessions for managers. Every setting is
different and rules must evolve to suit each setting,

evolution

not be imposed as an external prescription by the facilitator.

1. **Respect the person who 'holds the context'** at any point in a dialogue. There will be one (or perhaps more than one) person who is 'holding the context'; in an Action Learning 'set', for example, it is the 'problem-holder'. It is about keeping focus in the dialogue, treading a fine line between exploration and wandering off the point.

2. **Suspend your tendency to judge,** listen and try to understand, rather than focusing on what you might want to say in response to what is being said.

3. **Treat everyone's views as equally valid.** If this isn't done the dialogue will collapse as participants become aware of the inequalities.

When a group of people talk about an event they have experienced or heard about, they often generate a 'swarm' of different interpretations, which may or may not resonate with others' perceptions. Which views and ideas come to dominate people's thinking is determined almost randomly within the 'possibility space' of the dialogue; it is certainly non-linear in character, with tiny comments often having a disproportionately large effect on others. There is therefore a tension between what the individual wants to say to promote their own interests and the interests of the group.

perspectives/ 'AND-not-but'

An organisation which takes the time to listen to its customers will receive a wider range of perceptions and views than it might otherwise consider. When brought together, those views can point to service improvements which are more likely to sustain the product or service and be perceived as a real improvement by a group of customers.

 Cross-references
networks, self-organisation, perspectives, autopoiesis, possibility space

 References

John Brockman, *The Third Culture*, Simon & Schuster, New York, 1995, ISBN 0 684 80359 3

Robin Dunbar, *Grooming, Gossip and the Evolution of Language*, Faber, London, 1996, ISBN 0 571 17396 9

Kevin Kelly, *Out of Control: the New Biology of Machines*, Fourth Estate, 1994, ISBN 1 85702 308 0

Michael McMaster, *The Intelligence Advantage: Organising for Complexity*, Butterworth-Heinemann, 1996, ISBN 0 7506 9792 X

Peter Senge, *The Fifth Discipline Fieldbook*, Nicholas Brealey, 1994, ISBN 1 85788 0609

Memes

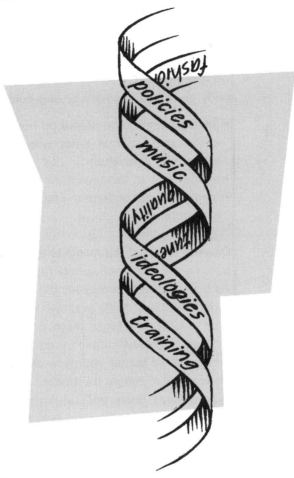

 ### Relevance

The idea of the meme is an attempt to explain the transmission of human culture. It is important to be aware of the constraints which memes impose on our attempts to create change, because we cannot control them; the best we can hope for is to influence their transmission.

Translation

*possibility
space*

What are memes?

Memes are the cultural equivalent of genes, and live in the 'possibility space' in our minds. Richard Dawkins, when he invented the concept, chose the word 'meme' because he wanted something that was reminiscent of both 'gene' and 'memory' to help convey three ideas:

- memes 'want' to be passed on from brain to brain, in the same way that genes 'want' to be passed on to the next generation
- memes 'live' in memory in our brains
- memes are not under our direct control, anymore than genes are.

Dawkins invented the meme to explain the transmission of human culture from person to person, via books, speech, television, and all the other communications media available. (The word 'culture' is used in a scientific broad sense, not in the narrow sense of 'highbrow culture' or art – in other words, all the aspects of human society or civilisation.) The sorts of elements of culture transmitted by memes could include: ideas, tunes, political slogans, policies, learning, education, training, fashions, stories, ideologies or jokes. All clichés are memes. Some more organisation-specific memes might be:

- quality
- value-for-money
- partnership
- stakeholder accountability
- learning organisation
- efficiency
- standards of competence
- customer focus
- business in the community
- doing more with less
- Business Process Re-engineering (BPR).

Memes will often look like 'soundbites': 'doing more with less' and 'value-for-money' are just the sort of phrases we hear politicians use in the media all the time (and the media is a 'playground' for memes). Yesterday's soundbites might become today's buzzwords and then tomorrow's clichés if they don't vanish immediately.

'Put the blame on meme'

What is Dawkins trying to tell us when he says that memes 'want' to be passed on from brain to brain, in the same way that genes 'want' to be passed on to the next generation? To answer this, we need to understand his idea of the 'selfish gene' – his great contribution to the genetics and evolution debate. He is asking us to do a mental 'flip' and look at reproduction, not from our viewpoint, which is the viewpoint of the organism, but from the gene's viewpoint. To ask: 'What's in it for the gene?' rather than: 'What's in it for the organism?' Obviously he is not saying that genes are **literally** selfish (although several of his critics wilfully misunderstood that), he is saying that genes act **as if** they are selfish. For example: ageing is obviously bad for the organism (you, or me), but from the point of view of our genes it might not make a lot of sense to keep us around wasting food after we've passed on our genes to the next generation – food that could be better used feeding that next generation. This is what he means by 'selfish gene': it is acting in its own best interest, not necessarily in the organism's best interest (although thankfully the two often coincide, or we'd all automatically die off once we had reproduced).

More specifically, Dawkins is saying that genes can be considered as 'replicators' – 'things which cause themselves to be copied'. The 'thing that is used to copy' is the 'vehicle'. He is saying that looking at genetics from the replicator's viewpoint may help explain more of the mysteries of genetics than the usual viewpoint which asks 'What's in it for the organism?' The table below gives some examples of replicators and the vehicles they use to replicate.

Replicators, vehicles and process

Replicator	Vehicle	Process
Gene	Organism	Reproduction
Egg*	Chicken*	Reproduction
Human genome	Human being – you	Reproduction
Meme	Human mind	Quasi-infection
Computer virus	Floppy disk	Magnetic data transfer

*A chicken is just an egg's way of making another egg

Modern biologists would tell you that the answer to the age-old question 'Which came first, the chicken or the egg?' is 'the egg'. This is because life first evolved as a self-organising soup of chemicals which developed replication before they developed the solid boundary to their system that we call 'the body'.

"When you plant a fertile meme in my mind you literally parasitise my brain, turning it into a vehicle for the meme's propagation in just the way that a virus may parasitise the genetic mechanism of a host cell."

Richard Dawkins, 1989

So memes are selfish: they don't necessarily care what happens to you, only that they transmit themselves. Depending on your viewpoint, you may see the memes in the list above as positive, negative, or neutral. As William Shaw observed in a profile of Michael Portillo, former UK Secretary of State for Defence: "The value of rumours lies not in their truth but in their viral transmittability."

Dawkins would obviously agree with Shaw, because Dawkins has always emphasised the selfishness of memes. Shaw's somewhat cynical view is that almost any rumour can aid his agenda as a 'spin-doctor': 'transmittability' being his only avowed criterion. (Incidentally a spin-doctor is an example of a 'memetic engineer'. If we have genetic engineering, why not memetic engineering? Politicians, spin-doctors, advertisers and even trainers are in the business of engineering memes to invade brains.)

Memetics

There is now a high level of interest in Dawkins' ideas, and a body of research has grown up under the title 'memetics'. 'Memeticists' have extended and modified the ideas, pointing out, for example, that memes use a different type of transmission to genes – one that is more like infection, or the action of enzymes in biochemistry. For example, in training departments we can observe that the meme 'standards of competence' is blocked by the meme 'but we're already doing that with National Vocational Qualifications (NVQs)'.

'Standards of competence' are the basis of NVQs: developed to reflect the work of an occupation, such as engineering or childcare. Many organisations are now using the same method to derive in-house 'standards of competence' for their organisation – an approach which has many advantages.

An example of meme selection and infection: Business Process Re-engineering (BPR)

"My boss went to the USA and caught the BPR bug."

A director of a British company in conversation with Ilfryn Price, Lecturer in Facilities Management, Sheffield Hallam University, UK

Price points out that in the early 90s BPR wasn't the only version of this particular meme around; he quotes the following variants: Business Process Review, Business Process Simplification, Business Process Management, Business Process Innovation, Business Process Improvement, Business Process Control, and Business Process Transformation.

increasing returns and lock-in

> *"The differences were more theoretical than significant. Now, five years later, we hear only the one term used. 'Re-engineering' triumphed, perhaps by contingency, as much as by design or inherent 'fitness'. It locked in adherents via positive feedback in a classic QWERTY dynamic. That dynamic – widespread proliferation and experimentation followed by stabilisation around one, or a few designs – is common if not universal in the introduction of new technologies."*
>
> Ilfryn Price

Application
A note of caution for the change-agent

If we accept Dawkins' idea, anyone attempting to change an organisation is involved in meme transmission by definition, because all ideas are memes, and all attempts to change organisations involve ideas.

> *"... when a CEO wants to transform a company, he or she must first change the language of that company."*
>
> Michael McMaster

It is therefore important to be aware of the constraints which memes can impose on our attempts to create change. Our efforts can backfire: one meme which had the opposite effect to that intended by its creator was the cartoonist Vicky's portrayal of Harold Macmillan as Superman. Intended to ridicule, the image of Supermac ended up being used in government publicity. Things will rarely turn out smoothly according to plan: ideas will be distorted, either by mistake or by the deliberate actions of vested interests; people will 'get hold of the wrong end of the stick', others won't listen, and others will misunderstand. Phrases like these will be heard:

"You're putting words into my mouth."

"Well said, that's a good way of putting it..."

"Haven't I heard that somewhere before?"

"What I'm trying to say is..."

In just the same way that we cannot control what our children will be like, because their genetic makeup results from random mixing of their parents' genes, we cannot control what memes are transmitted as a result of our actions. We need therefore to be very cautious as we attempt to make changes.

New meme, new danger
There are, however, examples of successful memetic change. Professor Hari Tsoukas, a political management theorist, describes how Margaret Thatcher had first to 'plausibly retell the story of Britain since the Second World War', in order to begin the process of implementing Thatcherism. Although Tsoukas does not use memetics overtly within his explanation, he has acknowledged the power of memes in the change process employed to bring about Thatcherism (private communication, 1996). Staying in the political arena, during the 1997 UK General Election, the meme 'New Labour' successfully embedded itself in the national culture. The counter-meme 'New Labour, New Danger'

autopoiesis

failed. The alert reader will have noticed headings elsewhere in this book, in addition to the pastiche within this heading, which are variants of this meme!

The book you are reading is an attempt to create a set of memes which will have positive effects on organisations and individuals by offering new perspectives and new ways of thinking. These new memes will have to survive the processes of organisational (natural) selection, competing against memes like the 'We've done all that before' meme and the 'Well, it's basically just the learning organisation stuff again isn't it…' meme.

Memes and change initiatives
A thorough understanding of the way memes propagate can assist almost any change initiative. However much we decry the era of the 'soundbite', we cannot escape the power of the short, snappy phrase which lodges itself in people's minds. But beware: the 'soundbite' will only work if it links to an interesting idea or set of ideas: a 'meme complex' in the jargon. Memes are relevant in any context where cultural transmission is important, for example:

- day-to-day communication (face-to-face, written, email, phone, fax, etc.)
- formal and informal reports
- presentations announcing new initiatives.

They are particularly relevant to training and development; indeed we can redefine the role of the trainer, particularly in a 'transmission teaching' context as 'meme transmitter'.

The items on the following list, collected by John Darwin of the UK's Sheffield Business School, can be

considered as 'blocking memes' dedicated to
neutralising in-coming memes.

24 ways to kill an idea:
a meme spotter's checklist

1. Ignore it
2. See it coming and dodge
3. Scorn it
4. Laugh it off
5. Praise it to death
6. Mention that it has never been tried
7. Prove that it isn't new
8. Observe that it doesn't fit with organisation policy
9. Mention what it will cost
10. 'Oh, we've tried that before'
11. Cast the right aspersion
12. Find a competitive idea
13. Produce twenty good reasons why it won't work
14. Modify it out of existence
15. Encourage doubt about ownership
16. Damn it by association of ideas
17. Try to chip bits off it
18. Make a personal attack on the originator
19. Score a technical knock-out
20. Postpone it
21. Let a committee sit on the idea
22. Offer to take lead responsibility for developing the idea
23. Generalise
24. Encourage the author to look for a better idea.
25. ......

Cross-references

perspectives, possibility space, metaphor, ecosystem, self-renewal, autopoiesis

 ## References

Richard Dawkins, *River Out of Eden*, Weidenfeld and Nicholson, 1995, ISBN 0 297 81540 7

Richard Dawkins, *The Selfish Gene*, Oxford University Press, 1989, ISBN 0 19 286092 5

Michael McMaster, *The Intelligence Advantage: Organising for Complexity*, Butterworth-Heinemann, 1996, ISBN 0 7506 9792 X

Ilfryn Price and Ray Shaw, 'The Learning Organisation Meme: Emergence of a Management Replicator, or Parrots, Patterns and Performance', in T. Campbell and V. Duperret-Tran, Eds, 1996, *Proceedings of the Third ECLO Conference*, Copenhagen

Ilfryn Price, 'Organisational Memetics?: Organisational Learning as a Selection Process', in *Management Learning*, 1995 26/3, pp299-318

Metaphor

trees

 Relevance

Metaphors help us to link ideas in new ways so that new knowledge can emerge. They are a powerful way of using language to engage with complexity.

Translation

"Aristotle took the use of metaphor to be evidence of a superior intellect."

The Oxford Companion to the Mind

NB: No distinction is made here between metaphor and analogy, because strict grammar is not our concern; for the purposes of discussion, 'analogy' will be seen as a 'softer' version of 'metaphor'.

"This place is a madhouse, it's going to be total chaos any day now..."

"An organisation is an ecosystem..."

"An organisation is like the human body..."

We are all familiar with metaphors (including mixed ones) from reading poetry, fiction and management literature, but they can also have powerful effects in our day-to-day interactions at work. Jerome Bruner in his book *Actual Minds, Possible Worlds*, points out that metaphors can greatly assist problem solving:

"The history of science is full of (metaphors). They are crutches to help us get up the abstract mountain. Once up, we throw them away, even hide them, in favour of a formal logically consistent theory..."

Jerome Bruner

Because the brain works by making comparisons, metaphors can be seen as the expression of those comparisons embodied in language. Metaphors help to reveal new knowledge by linking ideas together in a new way, and helping hidden ideas to emerge. For example, thinking about the immune system in the organisation's 'body' can generate new ideas about the role of a personnel department:

Fighting disease = Preventing abuses of employment practice

Metaphor

| Keeping the body healthy | = Promoting good practice, equalities |

but also

autopoiesis

| Resisting transplants | = Preventing healthy change in the organisation |

attractor, complex adaptive systems, ecosystem

Metaphors as attractors

Metaphors can work as 'attractors' pulling ideas together; they can be a powerful way of using language to deal with complexity. New metaphors can open up new thinking.

Elsewhere in this book, new metaphors for organisations and teams are suggested: the organisation as complex adaptive system; the organisation as an ecosystem.

Gareth Morgan analyses a series of metaphors which have been used to describe organisations in his book *Images of Organisation*, pointing out that metaphors can also be very restrictive. For example a 'cost centre' is a financial entity which, when used outside of its applicability, becomes a metaphor which exerts a negative effect on the thinking of service managers: it can become part of a mindset that sees all 'costs' as 'bad', and ignores 'value' or 'benefit'.

> "...many of our activities (arguing, solving problems, budgeting time, etc.) are metaphorical in nature. The metaphorical concepts that characterise those activities structure our present reality. New metaphors have the power to create a new reality."
>
> Lakoff and Johnson

Brian Arthur feels that a key role for the Santa Fé Institute is the development of new metaphors and a new vocabulary which can enrich our understanding of complex human systems. In Mitchell Waldrop's book *Complexity*, he describes the negative effects of the wrong metaphors:

> *"If you have a truly complex system, then the exact patterns are not repeatable. And yet there are themes that are recognisable. In history, for example, you can talk about 'revolutions', even though one revolution might be quite different from another. So we assign metaphors. It turns out that an awful lot of policy-making has to do with finding the appropriate metaphor. Conversely, bad policy-making almost always involves finding inappropriate metaphors. For example, it may not be appropriate to think about a drug 'war' with guns and assaults."*

perspectives

Michael Lissack argues that managers who can make use of the metaphors of complexity see their organisations in a different light to those who don't, and in a sense, are competing in a different world. He says that:

> *"Complexity research is not at the point of describing an underlying theory of everything. But its descriptive powers are at a point where they can help to shape the world around us. Meanings and metaphors matter. The meanings that we give to ourselves, our products, our competitors, our customers, and all the relevant others in our world determine the space of our possible actions and, to a large extent, how we act."*

Lissack offers the list in the following table as a guide to the application of complexity metaphors to the work of organisations.

Metaphor

Complexity metaphors in the work of organisations

Metaphorical concept	Inference	Practical application
Fitness landscape	Local vs. global optima	Search (for improvements) strategies
Fitness landscape	Coevolving deformations	Be aware of feedback loops and interactions with all levels of stakeholders
Attractor	Behaviour passively following a pattern	Choice is more important than trying to influence predestined behaviour
Simulated annealing	Use 'chaos' to control 'chaos'	A bit of bedlam can be a good thing for crowds, data flow, and information
Simulated annealing	'Noise' can add creativity	Seek out controlled elements of noise, new voices, and outside perspectives
Tau	Too much data causes a clogging of the pipes	Limit the quantity of simultaneous change which the organisation attempts to recognise
Generative relationships	Seek tomorrow's returns in each encounter today	Approach each encounter by asking 'How will this help me grow?'
Increasing returns	Knowledge-based components of economy differ from traditional ones	Promote network and community effects whenever possible
Sensitive dependence on initial conditions	Prediction is impossible	Control per se won't work

from Lissack 1996

 Application

Metaphors are relevant to any situation that requires both new thinking and reflection on past experience in order to reach a deeper understanding. When working with groups who may be suspicious of metaphors, it can be useful to start by focusing on their own experience of the organisation, **before** looking at metaphors and images. One less threatening approach would be to ask:

"If your organisation was a < * > of some kind what would it be? Say why you chose this description. Draw a picture to illustrate your ideas."

*slot in an appropriate word from the list: vehicle, building, character in a play, film or story, an animal or other living thing.

Guiding metaphors for staff development

The following table is based on group discussions at 'Navigating Complexity' workshops. New possibilities were opened up by the garden metaphor: for example, continuous improvement emerged naturally from thinking about staff development as a process of nurturing living things.

Mechanical	Biological
Organisation as factory	Organisation as garden
Staff development as 'annual maintenance'	Staff development as nurturing a plant
Needs monitoring from time to time	Needs constant interaction
Complicated system made up of simple systems	Complex adaptive system made up of complex adaptive systems
Essentially 'closed' system	Essentially 'open' system
Stays the same (but wears out)	Grows
Detailed procedural quality systems	Continuous improvement based on shared values

A similar exercise was carried out on a programme called 'Trainer as Leader' run by The Local Government Management Board for public sector managers and aimed at trainers wishing to take on a more strategic role in their organisations. This produced a stimulating and varied range of metaphors including ant colonies, a group struggling to climb a cliff, and a flotilla of small boats. Participants were able to explore the meaning of their personal experiences of organisational change through their personal metaphors. Both the individuals and the group learned much from this process of metaphor exploration.

 ## Cross-references
meme, perspectives, possibility space, ecosystem

 ## References

Lakoff, G., and Johnson, M., *Metaphors We Live By*, University of Chicago Press, 1995, quoted in Lissack, 1996

Michael R. Lissack, *Chaos and Complexity: What does that have to do with Management?*, unpublished 1996 paper available at his website: lissack.com/writings

Gareth Morgan, *Images of Organisation*, Sage, 1986, ISBN 0 80392 831 9

M. Mitchell Waldrop, *Complexity: the Emerging Science at the Edge of Order and Chaos*, Penguin, 1994, ISBN 0140179682

Receiver-based communication (RBC)

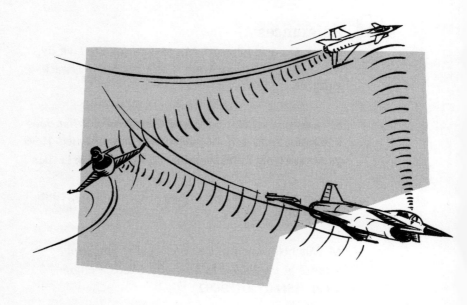

 Relevance

RBC is a key example of a communication system designed to take advantage of network possibilities.

Translation

When we think of communication we tend to think of one person talking to another, or we might think of a memo being sent down the hierarchy to make an announcement. We don't generally think of communication as everyone in a group telling everyone else in the group what is happening to them, all the time. But that is exactly what receiver-based communication is.

Stuart Kauffman describes receiver-based communication (RBC) as follows:

"All the agents in a system that is trying to co-ordinate behaviour, let other agents know what is happening to them. The receivers of this information use it to decide what they are going to do. The receivers base their decisions on some overall specification of 'team' goal."

There are moves afoot (or should we say in flight?) to abolish air traffic control and replace it with self-organisation. *Wired* magazine (2 April 1996) hosted an online discussion on 'Free Flight': a program that would equip individual aircraft with the technology to let them serve as their own air traffic controllers, increasing both flight efficiency and safety. "The technology exists. The only hurdles are the cost and the bureaucratic nature of the Federal Aviation Authority."

These are very general statements which should become clearer in a context. For example, the US Air Force uses RBC to allow groups of pilots to co-ordinate their behaviour in the absence of ground control. In a combat situation an 'air traffic control approach' would only make matters worse: top-down hierarchical communication cannot possibly deliver the information that each 'agent' needs when they need it.

The film 'Top Gun' contains several flight sequences which illustrate this. The pilots are constantly talking to each other, reporting what is happening to them ('He's

self-organisation

on my tail'), and choosing to concentrate on messages from those nearest to them. Thus they achieve collective co-ordination in a way loosely analogous to flocking behaviour in birds. This is an example of self-organising behaviour, but please note: the self-organisation is in the context of an overall goal: in 'Top Gun' it is to stop the 'bad guys'. This goal is set by the organisation of which the team is a part; the group is only free to self-organise within the context of the goal. This is very reminiscent of new management approaches to teamwork – in particular the 'self-managed team' approach.

New idea: do you copy?
RBC is also being used in companies; at the Xerox copier division, for example. When RBC was introduced as an experiment by consultants in the copier repair department, efficiency massively increased. Each engineer was given a 'walkie-talkie' set up permanently to receive all other messages. When an engineer heard someone else talking about something they were interested in they would start to pay close attention. The message might be a problem that someone was having ('How do I remove the cartridge mounting? They always seem to get jammed in place'), or equally a solution or suggestion ('Try tightening all the bolts first to release the locktite seal'). In this way, 'good practice' was able to spread rapidly through the entire repair shop.

It is important to note that all the communications are 'broadcast' to the whole group. There is no selection or filtering. The 'receiver' makes their own decision to act or not. As you might expect when the system was first introduced, messages tended to be the usual gossip and chat that people indulge in at coffee

Receiver-based communication (RBC)

dialogue,
autopoiesis

breaks. This is because engineers were not used to talking about work problems with each other; they tended to work alone, only very occasionally consulting other engineers. So their initial use of the system was one that they were familiar with: chat and gossip. They didn't really understand why management had introduced the radios. Management, supported by the consultants, had to hold back and trust that work-related messages would come to predominate.

Over the next few weeks, more and more messages were about repairs as people began to see the value of the system: increasing returns had started in a positive feedback loop.

The essence of RBC is that communication is networked across the team, not mediated by a hierarchy. The role of the hierarchy is to set the conditions and specify the goal; not to tell the team 'how to do it'.

An important part of setting the conditions is the 'legitimation' of gossip within the RBC system. Unfortunately middle management felt threatened by RBC and attempted to abolish it.

network and
hierarchy

To find out what happened see 'network emergence (and how to kill a network)' in 'network and hierarchy' (p.49).

fitness
landscape

The individual repair workers can also be viewed as 'patches' in the sense that Kauffman describes when discussing improving the 'fitness' of organisations.

Application

RBC is potentially applicable in a wide of range of teams or groups. It may be of particular relevance to 'self-regulated' teams. It applies in situations where:

- the individuals have similar or identical jobs
- there is a group
- there is a common goal
- the individuals have some autonomy in deciding how their actions will contribute to the goal (methods and procedures are not rigidly specified)
- there are complex, conflicting issues
- specific solutions can only be found by the individuals.

Cross-references

dialogue, autopoiesis, increasing returns, network and hierarchy, self-organisation, fitness landscape

References

Stuart Kauffman, *At Home in the Universe*, Oxford University Press, 1995, ISBN 0 195095995

Michael R. Lissack, *Chaos and Complexity: What does that have to do with Management?*, unpublished 1996 paper available at his website: lissack.com/writings

Perspectives

 Relevance

To engage with complexity, we need perspectives which admit the possibility that more than one thing can be true at once.

Translation
Mindset

When I chat to someone over samosas and warm chicken legs at a seminar lunch, and I don't know who they are, my view of them will change in some way if I discover that the person is a chief executive, and equally if I discover that she is knowledgeable about complexity theory, or uses a Macintosh computer.

Multiple truths

*perspectives/
'AND-not-but'*

When an old friend turns up just as I'm rushing out of the house my mind will struggle with two seemingly incompatible views: am I pleased to see her or is it a nuisance because I've got to go out? (It can be both.)

Different rationalities

I actually enjoy cycling in London **and** I hate commuting into London by train. You may hold the opposite view. I make decisions in a way that makes sense to me but not necessarily to you. It depends on your point of view – we all look at things from our own viewpoint.

So what?

Why is any of this important or relevant? In a nutshell, an undeniably complex world demands an unequivocally complex worldview: "The world is divided into two sorts of people: those who think that the world is divided into two sorts of people, and those who think it is more complicated than that" (attributed to Oscar Wilde).

*memes,
dialogue*

Michael McMaster suggests that the intelligence of corporations is bound up in the language they use to describe and function in their world.

"Our greatest obstacle in exploring ideas of complexity and complex systems is that we do not experience our world as occurring in language. For us, the world just 'is'. And the way it 'just is' is the way in which our language of linear, materialistic systems represents it to us."

Michael McMaster

Perspectives: different views of the world

The way that I view the world is not the same as the way that you view the world. We have different **perspectives**. And the way that I view the world when I'm in a team meeting, or when making a presentation to colleagues, or listening to a colleague make one, or just in conversation, is not the same. I myself view the world in a subtly different way in each different setting. And when I reflect on one of those earlier interactions at home later the same day, my world view will be subtly different again. If I'm a manager, my view of my team meeting may well be very different from that of my team members, both singly and as a group, yet we all may have exactly the same view of the fascinating presentation made by a colleague from another department. We can have, and do have, many different perspectives on the many different arenas in which we perform; some of them seemingly contradictory and inconsistent.

Raining ideas

Dr Ilfryn Price provides a new perspective on the development of our mental perspectives.

"A geological metaphor provides an image of the physiology and psychology of memes at work upon the individual or collective mind. Imagine a landscape, eroded over time to provide streams, rivulets, and rivers interspersed between higher plateaux. It provides a simple

example of a self-organising, locked-in, system. Over time, accumulations of rainfall carve out stream and river beds and settle into pools and lakes. Any new rainfall will no longer find its own way but will rather take, and re-inforce, the already sculpted path of least resistance. Though the falling rain may be evenly distributed across the land, in its collection and flow across the landscape, it will tend towards a pre-determined route taken by previous rainfalls.

Just as the rainfall follows established routes, so perception follows established ways of 'seeing'. Technically, even if the light sources which perturb the back of the retina, or the acoustic waves the eardrum, are identical, what will be noticed from all that could be seen or heard will depend on the perceptual lens through which we view the world. What is there is not independent of the receiver. What is there is what we have been 'trained' (or conditioned or have learnt) to 'see'. We may discard, indeed we can be blind to, anomalies that do not fit. The self-organised pattern which we call our thinking grants a particular perceptual blindness and rigidity to our perceptions of the world.

memes

Exploring the analogy further we could say that an idea, a single thought, an utterance – a meme in fact – is like the single raindrop. It falls upon a pre-formed perceptual 'memescape'. Isolated thoughts gather together in a string – a pattern of co-existing memes – which we might compare to a few drops congregating together in a splash of water. With sufficient mass the splash of water starts to flow into streams and rivers which are, if we like, the connectors between the raindrops and the pools and lakes, if not the oceans, of our thoughts. The pools and lakes we may view as concept pools and theory lakes. Thus, a self-organising system is inherited and developed in which the flow of perception takes a certain course; it follows a certain pattern, a largely given paradigm.

attractor,
fitness
landscape

*Patterns in companies, habits and rules of behaviour,
codes of thinking, systems of language, states of
relationship coalesce in similar fashion around shared
'landscapes of perception'."*

The need to understand our models of reality

*"Each of us has acquired from our society a conceptual
model of reality. The most important task of general
education is to help us understand that model, the models
of those with whom we interact, and the range of
alternative models from which we might choose."*

Marion Brady in a posting to the Learning Organisation email
discussion group

Brady might equally have added that this is the most
important task in the training of 'public service' staff in
order that they may deal with the unique complexities
of their work. In the pages that follow, several aspects
of 'perspectives' are explored.

Management and the 'modern paradigm'

John Darwin, Senior Lecturer in Strategic Management
at Sheffield Business School, has written extensively on
the 'modern paradigm'. In these extracts, the
terms 'paradigm', 'mindset', 'perspective' and
'worldview' are all used to explore aspects of
the way we view and act in the world. Aspects
of the modern paradigm and its impact on
management are explored.

[Please note: the material
below, taken from Darwin's
unpublished 1995 paper
The Wisdom Paradigm, has
been given new headings
and has also been edited
for length.]

Darwin suggests that management theory and
practice has been dominated by an amalgam of
ideas taken primarily from economics and the
philosophy of science which together constitute
what he calls the modern paradigm. This has its
roots in the Cartesian-Newtonian scientific paradigm.

Management mindset: the 'dominant logic'

Prahalad and Bettis have set out their views of management mindset in two papers on the 'dominant logic'. In the first, they argue:

> *"Few organisational events are approached by these managers (or any managers) as being totally unique and requiring systematic study. Instead, they are processed through pre-existing knowledge systems... A dominant general management logic is defined as the way in which managers conceptualise the business and make critical resource allocation decisions... The dominant logic is stored via schemas and hence can be thought of as a structure."*

In their second paper, Prahalad and Bettis extend their discussion. They relate it first to the huge amounts of information available to managers as a result of information technology.

> *"What is [actually] seen [...] are information-rich but interpretation-poor systems. In other words, systems that seem to confuse raw information or data with appropriate actionable knowledge."*

They continue:

> *"We have come to view the dominant logic as an information filter. Organisational attention is focused only on data deemed relevant by the dominant logic. Other data are largely ignored. [...] The dominant logic puts constraints on the ability of the organisation to learn. In other words, it is a primary determinant of organisational intelligence."*

complex adaptive systems

Prahalad and Bettis also usefully link their concept of dominant logic to the concept of complex adaptive systems. They see the dominant logic as an adaptive emergent property of complex organisation.

"Work on systems far from equilibrium is suggestive of conditions that facilitate unlearning. Complex systems near equilibrium tend to form in a repetitive fashion. As Prigonine, Stengers and others point out, when such a system is in equilibrium, it acts as though it is 'blind'. Its behaviour becomes repetitive. However, as it moves too far from equilibrium states, it becomes 'able to perceive', to 'take into account' in its way of functioning, differences in the external world."

'Multivalued logic'

One important feature of the modern paradigm, which stretches back at least to the time of Aristotle, is the use of bipolar, crisp logic – the 'either/or' approach which has dominated Western thinking for more than two millennia. Occasionally we are exhorted to transcend this with 'both/and'; occasionally this is represented as a key facet of Eastern thinking (and hence as contributing to the post-war economic success of countries such as Japan). The desire to polarise and establish antonyms is strong – it is to be seen in precisely this dichotomy between Western and Eastern thought. Just as Newtonian physics may be seen as a special case of the physics of Einstein, applicable only in certain circumstances, so the 'either/or' logic of the modern paradigm is just one part of the 'multivalued logics' applicable in contexts of great unpredictability.

Rationality

Managers, like most people, like to appear as rational beings. Rationality, in turn, is seen as synonymous with being logical (other terms managers might use include sensible, methodical, rigorous, systematic …). Herbert Simon famously described this as 'bounded rationality'; his idea was that there are severe constraints on the administrator's ability to make rational decisions such as

*fitness landscape/
good enough*

metaphor

conflicts of interest, lack of data, etc. In keeping with the comments of the previous paragraph, this form of rationality can be seen as somewhat restricted. The use, for example, of paradox, will not be seen as irrational, but rather as an expansion of more traditional ways of thinking. In the same way, the use of metaphor can be seen as a way of expanding our ideas.

Rationality: 'It's logical, Captain'
'Management science' has sought to be just that: a science. Theorists have therefore sought to analyse the nature of natural science, and in particular its method, to find parameters and principles for adoption in their own work. At the same time, the influence of that social science seen as closest to natural science – economics – has been substantial, and this has been reinforced by the influence over the last decade of the 'competitive positioning' approach to strategy. It is therefore possible to suggest that three types of 'ideal person' underpin modern management thinking (most of the writings would refer to these as 'ideal men', but an ungainly turn of phrase is preferred to a sexist one). These are: the 'rational person', the 'economic person' and the 'scientific person'.

The 'rational person' is characterised by the property of perfect knowledge, and the ability to obtain and retain perfect information. Also it is assumed that:

• at work, people are always rational and logical
• all else being equal, decisions are always about selecting the best alternative.

The myth of the economic person is that the market is perfect, free and open, and everyone behaves perfectly within it. Similarly, the myth of the scientific person tells us that our decisions are always logical, perfectly quantified, based on an understanding of cause and effect, and carried out in our mind, without any influence from our body, i.e. free from emotions, and other distractions, like Mr. Spock in 'Star Trek'.

These assumptions are the basis of 'modern' management, which came into being with F.W. Taylor, and they are all highly questionable.

Paradigms and the 'world perspective'

John Darwin explains two related ideas: the concept of 'world perspective' which is rooted in language, and 'paradigm' which is a set of preconceptions about the world.

> *"The world perspective is a function of two factors. On the one hand, it depends on the material of experience, which is its foundation; on the other hand, it depends on the conceptual apparatus, and the meaning rules that are bound up with it. A change in conceptual apparatus is reflected in a change in the problems which one solves on the basis of the same data of experience. Different scientists make use of different conceptual structures which can only partially coincide. But even one and the same science changes its conceptual apparatus in the course of its historical development. This change, however, is often concealed by the fact that while the concepts are changed, the words remain the same."*
>
> Darwin quoting K. Ajdukiewicz on 'world perspective'

There are several important elements here. First, while the world perspective affects, indeed determines, the boundaries of behaviour, it is fundamentally based in language. Second, changes in the perspective can be hard to identify because the language may not change substantially while the concepts within it do. This theory implies that it may be possible to choose two different types of conceptual apparatus in such a way that, from the same evidence, two radically different world perspectives may be formulated, both fully compatible with that evidence because that is how it is interpreted.

This relates back to the discussion on rationality, for it implies that there will be different interpretations of what is rational depending on how that and related concepts are formulated within each world perspective.

There are also implications for management, since it challenges many of the approaches and ideas which rely on the belief that there can be a single perspective, and a single concept of rationality: these include notions of common culture, common values, and the management of resistance to change.

"The culture of any group of people is that set of beliefs, customs, practices and ways of thinking that they have come to share with each other through being and working together. It is a set of assumptions people simply accept without question as they interact with each other. At the visible level, the culture of a group of people takes the form of ritual behaviour, symbols, myths, stories, sounds, and artifacts."

Professor Ralph Stacey, University of Hertfordshire, UK

In this sense, culture is part of a shared world perspective, and will therefore be shared only in so far as the world perspective is shared.

Stacey has defined the paradigm as follows:

"A paradigm is the set of preconceptions we bring from our past to each new situation we have to deal with. The paradigm is, as it were, the lens through which we look at the world and it therefore determines what we perceive. A paradigm is a set of beliefs or assumptions we make about the world, normally beneath the level of awareness and therefore mostly never questioned. As we live and work with other people, we come to share a particular way of focusing on the world and that shared paradigm determines what explanations we develop and agree upon amongst ourselves."

This is helpful, but note that it is not as rich as the approach taken by Ajdukiewicz, who recognises the central role of language and the extent to which the world perspective embraces method and conscious thinking. Indeed one could go further: the closely related Sapir-Whorf hypothesis argues that each language has its own metaphysics. This is more in line with the definition given by Fritjof Capra:

Grateful acknowledgement is given to John Darwin for the use of the above material.

"The totality of thoughts, perceptions, and values that forms a particular vision of reality, a vision that is the basis of the way a society organises itself."

A new perspective on perspectives

Onar Åm is developing a new philosophy to facilitate dealing with multiple perspectives. He describes it as follows:

"Perspectivism is about consolidating fundamentally different paradigms and philosophies. The consolidation is not limited to incommensurate world views but also to strongly rivaling – maybe even contradicting – perspectives. This has a tendency of confusing people. I often hear statements like, 'You can't adhere to both X and Y. You have to choose'. Perspectivism is about realising the limitations of

perspectives and that one perspective may be powerful where another one fails and vice versa. Perspectivism also means to realise that contradictions between perspectives are often superficial and created by their intrinsic limitations."

Onar Åm

 Application
Rationality and management in the public sector
In his paper *Diamond Thunderbolt Management*, John Darwin, Senior Lecturer in Strategic Management at Sheffield Business School, and ex-head of Economic Development for Sheffield City Council, looks at theory and practice in local government.

He states that:

"There is strong pressure on managers to be rational – perhaps even more on public sector managers than those in the private sector, because of the public scrutiny to which their actions are subjected."

He goes on to discuss the roots of this rationality, (the 'management and the modern paradigm' entry above explores some of the key areas) then concludes that:

"The rational analytic approach to strategic management is premised on the Cartesian-Newtonian thinking, [...] still valuable in a reductive environment where problems can be isolated and given a 'value-free' flavour (which is to say where a single set of values are predominant). However, this is rarely the case in the public sector – and perhaps decreasingly so in the private sector – as we move towards stakeholder approaches which involve multiple value systems. Such complexity is also apparent in the increasingly important context of inter-organisational situations, including partnerships, joint ventures, strategic alliances, network organisations and organisational clusters."

Different rationalities

Robert Hughes, a UK public sector Chief Executive, presents a slightly different view of rationality, emphasising that there is not one single rationality. Instead he asserts that there are a number of 'different rationalities' at play in the work of organisations. He singles out two others in particular that should be given a place alongside the trio of technical/professional, economic, and legal rationality in the work of a local government organisation: 'social rationality' and 'political rationality'.

In the three rationalities, we focus on objectives and single goals: the engineer designs the best stadium, while the economist seeks optimisation in the use of resources. These rationalities are based on expertise, standardisation and routine. Professionals focus on single issues like education or social services, not broad issues of social cohesion or the environment. It is, of course, important that local government organisations continue to operate within these rationalities: they are vital to the well-being of people both in the organisations and in the communities in which they exist; for example, without legal rationality we would have no certainty about being paid for our work or receiving a pension when we retire.

Hughes describes political rationality as the rationality of power; it's about the arguments for doing 'expeditious things'. Politics is a social as well as hierarchical activity; it is the rationality of decision-making, influence and negotiation. This isn't problematic in a single organisation, but in inter-organisational settings you can find that the power you thought you had has evaporated like a will-o'-the-wisp.

He gives a graphic illustration of the power of social rationality: a man is walking through the park with his five children. He is unemployed, his wife is ill and he has no money. One of his children falls in the lake. What should he do?

The technically rational thing for him to say is: "I'm on the dole. My wife is ill. I've got lots of hungry mouths to feed. I'll be better off with one less child, so I'll let him drown."

We would think him insane (and criminal) if he did. We know what he actually does: he jumps into the lake to save the child, risking drowning and leaving his wife and kids even more impoverished. Why? According to Hughes this is because of social rationality (what we could call the 'the rationality of caring') which often overrides the rationality of logic. Social rationality links to the other rationalities in some ways – for example, it can be seen as sensible in terms of the survival of society – because without the caring instinct, the family unit is threatened, and without the family unit, our society and the survival of our species are threatened. It is possible (if we wanted to see it that way) that as the father jumps in the lake, he is thinking legally – he will rescue the child to avoid prosecution. Or he could be thinking economically – this child will look after me in my old age. But the central issue – which has nothing to do with others – is about being part of the human family in the broadest sense. Our Western industrialised society takes us away from these uncomfortable things, but we ignore them at our peril. Hughes argues that it is **possible** to run an organisation by being just a good bureaucrat, a good manager or a leader who makes things happen, without being human, but it is not sustainable in the longer term. We need a balanced approach: as managers we must include social rationality in our approach to our work.

'AND-not-but': a key tool for handling multiple perspectives

In a climate of diverse customer needs, we need ways to handle multiple perspectives. 'AND-not-but' is one such method. Consider the following scenario:

When an old friend knocks on the door, and we're about to rush out, we tend to say something like:

"Oh, hello Jill, it's really nice to see you *but* I'm just off out to the pictures, I'm meeting Jack at 8 outside the Odeon. Be seeing you. Can you call round tomorrow?"

(Or if we're not in a particularly good mood, we might vary it slightly by saying:

"Oh, hello Jill, I'm just off out to the pictures, I'm meeting Jack at 8 outside the Odeon, *but* it's really nice to see you. Must dash." Which seems a bit less friendly.)

Now this isn't what we mean; or rather it isn't *everything* that we mean, because both statements can be true:

• Statement 1: It's really nice to see you.
• Statement 2: I'm just off out to the pictures.

We are pleased to see our friend, *and* we do have to go out. Using 'AND-not-but' is a way of expressing two true statements which can *appear* to be contradictory. We say *appear* because, if we examine them, the two statements don't have to be negated by each other. If we met walking down the street, and we were both walking in the direction of the cinema, then it is clear that there is no conflict between the two statements; they are just two elements of a conversation. So restating the ideas, this time using 'AND-not-but':

"Oh, hello Jill, it's really nice to see you *and* I'm just off out to the pictures, I'm meeting Jack at 8 outside the Odeon."

The other person can hear the difference in your words, and can therefore appreciate the difference in meaning: they can hear that you are *both* pleased to see them *and* that you have to go out, two truths which aren't contradictory.

'AND-not-but' has a good scientific pedigree. In quantum mechanics there is a phenomenon known as the 'wave-particle duality' which is the physicists' version of 'both things are true'. Sometimes light behaves as if it is a wave; at other times it behaves like a particle. When light bends in water, it's behaving like a wave, but when it hits a solar cell it behaves like a particle: each single photon (the name of the light particle) 'knocks' a single electron off in the solar cell, generating electric current. So is light a particle or a wave? It's both: wave and particle are just two different viewpoints, two aspects of a bigger truth, just like 'I'm going out' and 'I'm pleased to see you'.

Cross-references

attractor, fitness landscape, dialogue, memes, possibility space

References

Onar Åm, *Perspectivism*, unpublished 1994 paper available at his website:
http://www.stud.his.no/~onar/

John Darwin, 'Diamond Thunderbolt Management', in *Teaching Public Administration*, Spring 1996, Volume XVI, No.1, pp 76-88

John Darwin, *The Wisdom Paradigm*, Sheffield Business School, unpublished paper, 1995

Robert Hughes, presentation to the Tools for Learning workshop in Huddersfield, UK, 6 February 1996

Michael McMaster, *The Intelligence Advantage: Organising for Complexity*, Butterworth-Heinemann, 1996, ISBN 0 7506 9792 X

Ilfryn Price and Ray Shaw, *Shifting the Patterns: Transforming the Codes of Personal and Company Performance*. (For further details contact the Harrow Partnership, Pewley Fort, Pewley Hill, Guildford, Surrey GU1 3SP, UK)

Ilfryn Price and Ray Shaw, 'The Learning Organisation Meme: Emergence of a Management Replicator, or Parrots, Patterns and Performance', in T. Campbell and V. Duperret-Tran, Eds, 1996, *Proceedings of the Third ECLO Conference*, Copenhagen

Possibility space

 ## Relevance
When change is constant, creativity and adaptation are crucial. Possibility space can embrace complexity: it is both a search strategy and a design strategy for the creation of possibilities.

Translation

*"Even today, when an Aboriginal mother notices the first stirrings of speech in her child, she lets it handle the 'things' of that particular country: leaves, fruit, insects and so forth. We give our children guns and computer games, **they** give their children the land."*

Bruce Chatwin

"The ability to explore the space of possibility can be found in an organisation's ability to engage in dialogue."

Michael McMaster

Possibility space is real

The concept of possibility space is derived, by way of complexity science, from the mathematical concept of a 'search space', a space in which the solutions to equations may be located in a three-dimensional graphical form.

metaphor

Possibility space is the place where all our ideas live before they are brought into being. Possibility space is real in the same way that an organisation is real: it is created in language. It is an extended metaphor for both the exploration of possibilities and the design of space for the creation of possibilities.

'Fitness landscape' is another space metaphor in complexity theory. A fitness landscape is a mountainous terrain showing the locations of the global maximum (highest peak) of fitness and the global minimum (lowest valley). One could say that fitness landscapes exist in a hilly part of possibility space.

fitness landscape

"Every human act takes place in language."

Humberto Maturana and Francisco Varela

The world we inhabit is constructed in language. For example, in Western society, marriage is still a key part of the world we live in. Not everyone is married, yet we all live in a world that sometimes appears obsessed with marriage.

Marriage is defined in language – the special language of the law – and is sustained in language. We use language to settle our differences and to express our feelings for each other. Language can also destroy a marriage: the things we say to each other can be enough to shatter the agreement in language that is a marriage.

In the same way, an organisation is constructed and maintained in language. The main activity of managers is talking, listening and conversation: creating and maintaining a shared world in language. In a very powerful sense, therefore, an organisation can be said to exist 'in language': an organisation is a set of ideas.

Imaginary boundaries in the real space of possibility
When we 'explore' ideas, we are exploring possibility space. This is more than just an analogy; it is a description of a **search process** which takes place in the mind. Normally when we search possibility space, we search only a tiny, familiar part of it, like a child that only plays in the park behind its house, never exploring further afield. There are certain places that the child is forbidden to go, and there are certain places that the child **thinks** it is forbidden to go. As the child is constrained by its parents, we are constrained both by the rules of our organisation and the rules we **imagine**

perspectives

for the organisation: these joint constraints are the limits of our perspective or world view. There are whole expanses of ideas which are possible, but we do not think about them because 'that isn't the sort of thing we do around here'. Now it may be true that certain ideas **are** frowned upon, or it may be merely that we are allowing a self-censoring process to operate on our thinking. Either way, if we deny ourselves access to a part of possibility space, we deny ourselves the possibility of finding new and useful ideas. It is a fear of

the 'edge of chaos'

what might happen if we cross the boundary into chaos; but if we never venture out from the zone of predictability, we can never discover those new ideas.

Possibility space

The zone of possibility and the zone of predictability

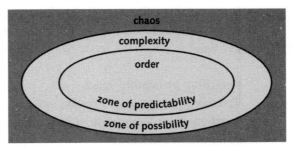

Adapted from Michael McMaster's book *The Intelligence Advantage*

Language that opens up possibilities

McMaster argues that traditional linear approaches to language see it as something that is used to **describe reality**. When language is based on a complex, open-ended perspective, there is room for expression, creativity and freedom. When used this way, language does not pin down thinking; instead it opens up the possibility space and helps to **bring forth reality**.

dialogue

The key mechanism is within conversation, specifically dialogue. Bringing forth reality can only be a shared activity in a group. My view of the possibilities is only one small part of the total; when augmented by your view and the views of others in our 'community' we can massively expand our possibility space.

Two views of what is possible

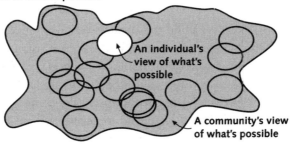

Adapted from Michael McMaster's book *The Intelligence Advantage*

Language gets its power in human systems, not from the accuracy with which it describes the world, but from its capacity to invent and continually re-invent the ways in which we relate to our shared worlds.

Searching possibility space

The word 'search' covers a wide range of ideas, and the word 'range' is appropriate; it evokes the idea of searching in a landscape – 'a range'. Before humans had language, searches could only take place in space in the real world: looking for food, or looking for shelter. Language enables us to search in possibility space, where we can range far and wide with great ease. All 'complex adaptive systems' engage in constant searching, be they economies or organisations, ecosystems or individual organisms. The term 'environmental scanning', one of the core competences of a good manager according to business schools, embodies a small part of the broad idea of the concept of searching possibility space.

complex adaptive systems

Application

You are now entering possibility space

When you start to discuss new approaches with a group, you can open up access to possibility space, or you can block it. Try to avoid existing 'linear' language because it does not allow the emergence of new possibilities. For example: try asking the question, 'How can we **grow** improvements?' rather than, 'How do we **build** this quality initiative?' A word like 'grow' will be unexpected in the context of your discussion – it is analogous to a large jump in a fitness landscape – and will help to nudge the discussion into new areas. When we use a phrase like the 'service delivery chain', it is literally a 'linear' metaphor which 'locks the discussion in' to the metaphor of chains and 'locks out'

fitness landscape

evolution of co-operation

perspectives/ 'AND-not-but', autopoiesis

increasing returns and lock-in

the possibility of a 'service delivery network' – a concept that may better encompass the interconnectedness of service delivery. The CEOs of Xerox and SmithKline Beecham have been quoted in the *Harvard Business Review* as saying 'process gives more freedom'. Their words should remind us that we are trying to design a set of processes for emergence, not a set of linear processes for control.

Managers as safari guides

Consider a typical discussion in a meeting at work. If someone is keen to make their point, they will tend not to listen to other people's views for fear of being seen as supporting others rather than proposing their own points. In this climate, many of the statements made by participants will be heard as contradictory, as individuals jockey for position in what they are perceiving as a 'win-lose' game. If an 'AND-not-but' approach is used instead, it allows individuals to make their points without negating the contributions of others. 'AND-not-but' is about opening up the possibility space, rather than closing it down. So the job of the manager or facilitator is to open up the possibility space in a discussion; to be the safari guide on an exploration of the landscapes of possibility.

A tip for travellers

Michael McMaster makes a general point about the design of what we are calling here 'possibility spaces', which is to 'take the position' – 'try it on to see what you get'. It's about 'provisionality' and uncertainty; there isn't a right way or an 'only way'. By making a provisional proposal to a group about how they might work together, new insights and new openings for action can emerge. (This also applies to the new ideas for the design itself.)

Designing possibility space

Michael McMaster describes the process (or rather one possible process out of many) as follows:

"If emergence is a valid term of cause and effect, then how can we design the spaces in which it will occur? Communication can be seen independently of individual senders and receivers (and even independent of acts of sending and receiving) and as something that occurs in the space between people – and that space can be designed for great effect.

If we approach the question as being about 'senders and receivers' then we'll have to concern ourselves with choosing the right ones, getting their intentions right, teaching them better communication skills, etc. If we approach the question as designing space, we need much less concern for who shows up. Those who show up at a pool hall or a concert will tend to get what they came for.

By inviting a group to a meeting (face-to-face, electronic, or other) where the invitation states the purpose and the process, by holding the meeting in a space that is appropriate to the purpose and process, by displaying the rules of the meeting and by supplying a facilitator, for example, I count on the intended results of the meeting being realised. (With the background assumption that the intended results were appropriate to the process and emergent nature of communication.)"

The issue of 'senders and receivers' is explored in the autpoietic model of communication in 'autopoiesis'

autopoiesis

Michael McMaster in a posting to the Learning Organisation email discussion group

Here's looking at you, sir
McMaster offers a concrete example. A
union/management dispute was closing a plant down
and the main participants had not communicated
successfully for years.

> "I got the general manager to invite the managers and the
> union executive to a meeting to consider a plan for
> transforming the relationships at the plant. When they
> arrived, I set a single ground-rule which they had either to
> accept or they would have to leave the meeting. The rule
> was: 'You will follow the process instructions that I give.'
> They all agreed. The first process rule was that they should
> not do anything for themselves (like getting coffee) but
> instead they should ask that someone 'from the other side'
> do it for them. Then, after a brief talk and introductions, I
> had them sit in 'mixed' pairs and just look at each other.
> Then they were asked to say a bit about what it was like at
> work for them, with a lot of silence and 'being with each
> other' in between.

> This meeting created a breakthrough in communication
> which persisted and was the beginning of a programme
> which transformed the plant.

> Anybody that has had successful large group meetings has
> seen miracles happen and knows that it comes from the
> design of the space and not from the individuals in the
> room. Those of us who do this kind of thing each have our
> own design of space for doing it.

> It is all about designing relationships. That is the kind of
> space that I'm referring to. That is, it's not 'empty space'
> with no awareness of what isn't 'empty'. The space being
> referred to is that space which is created by the
> relationship of things. This is not so much between those
> things as it is created by those things. This is the nature of
> communication itself. That is, if a sentence has a

'hardwired' meaning, then there is no room for emergence and minimum information is contained in that sentence. (It is unlikely that there is any such sentence but there are many that are close once the context is known.) Sentences like these are trivial, in my view, compared to all those which have much more possibility of generation, creativity, exploration and information."

Michael McMaster in a posting to the Learning Organisation email discussion group

Some principles for possibility space design
These ideas are based on various 'postings' by contributors to the Learning Organisation email discussion group.

Possibility space design: objectives
Not all objectives are appropriate; the following are examples which will be in harmony with the possibility space approach:

- to deliver practical support to people in the workplace
- to encourage a learning orientation to the challenges they face
- to provide tools that work to facilitators (people whose job is to support others to become more effective)
- to enhance the quality of thinking before action is taken.

Possibility space design: key elements of the process
- an 'organic growth' approach
- conscious (and public) experimentation
- start where there is interest: initially work only with those team managers that express interest
- support process to introduce and underpin the approach

- iterate the design process: produce a draft plan for the next few steps (stepping stones) then constantly review and amend it
- communicate results and achievements.

The 'search conference': a guided tour of possibility space

'Future search' is the most well-known of the 'search conference' methodologies which are available. A typical application of search conferencing is shown below; this time in a manufacturing context:

> *"My plan is to gather a variety of stakeholders who would otherwise never meet (line mechanics to department managers to outside suppliers) to discuss common issues about improving certain aspects of component quality in conjunction with customer service, collaboration, and team work."*
>
> From a posting to the Learning Organisation email discussion group

The 'future search' methodology was developed by Marvin Weisbord and Sandra Janoff in the US from the pioneering work of Frederick Emery in the UK; it is an example of a structured approach to the problem of developing new ideas and possibilities with large groups, and varied stakeholders.

The 'future search' process

Future search offers a model for achieving collaboration in organisations and communities. Participants are drawn from a 'whole system', within an organisation or community. They work together to review the past, focus on the present and 'mind-map' everyone's perspectives and views onto flipcharts, so that everything is public.

system, perspectives

Everyone's experience and perspectives are valued, and people take responsibility for their contribution to the problems and the solutions as they see them. The focus then shifts to the future and the barriers that need to be overcome to create the common ground on which everyone can play their part.

'Mind-mapping' is a technique, popularised by Tony Buzan, for linking interconnected ideas diagrammatically.

Future search is about:

• personal responsibility
• seeking out underlying simplicities
• confronting and absorbing complexity
• using dialogue to ensure everyone is heard
• tasks being worked on publicly
• putting co-ordination and control in the hands of participants
• engaging the whole person.

Future search and communities: extract from a proposal
Below is a description of a community in a large city, taken from a local government memo recommending the use of future search. It illustrates the sorts of issues that are potentially amenable to the future search approach.

"From the discussions we have had so far, I get the impression that the Belle Vue community is fragmented, somewhat transient, and although it feels anxious and fearful about its future, cannot seem to get the help it needs. There appear to be many different ideas and diverse interests at work, which are making it difficult to organise for joint community action. The absence of substantial investment resources doesn't help, of course. I also assume that if the solution was straightforward it would have been found by now. The community seems to have a long social and political

Possibility space

history which has dinted people's confidence and their hope that better times can lie ahead. It is obviously important not to raise any expectations that cannot be realised. We are looking for a catalyst which will commit everyone to change and find the common ground on which all the community's stakeholders can work together. It appears that the 'top-down' approaches by themselves are not working, and a 'bottom-up' initiative is needed to support them. It's vital that we do not see them as 'either/or' and 'us/them' issues. New patterns of interaction are needed which can deliver new hope, creative ideas and a shared responsibility for what emerges. People who don't normally get a chance to listen to each other need a chance to talk informally and find some common ground."

Below are some comments from another future search initiative focusing on housing issues. They give an insight into the process.

"Whose problem is housing really?"

"We have had to look at housing in a broader context and involve more people in the issue. We couldn't fall back on any of our old tools. We had to sit there and practice in the future search what we hoped to implement in the real world. Every voice is valid. We can't impose our stereotypes. We can't assume that we know the best way."

"Expect to hang-out in confusion. It's like a jigsaw puzzle with pieces that may feel overwhelming. The road to renewal often leads through denial and confusion."

"There is no need for anyone to change their mind, or anybody else's, for us to be successful. You need not give up your beliefs, values, and commitments."

"I think there is some disagreement here. That's fine by me."

"We are going to develop a network of stakeholders on employment and education with the emphasis on community issues."

"The map helped everyone see their community through different eyes. It gives you an appreciation of the complexity. You realise you can't handle everything at once."

 ## Cross-references

complex adaptive systems, fitness landscape, memes, metaphor, autopoiesis, perspectives, systems

 ## References

Tony Buzan, *The Mind Map Book*, BBC, 1993, ISBN 0 563 86373 8

Bruce Chatwin, *The Songlines*, Picador, ISBN 0 330 30082 2

Humberto Maturana and Francisco Varela, *The Tree of Knowledge: the Biological Roots of Human Understanding*, Shambhala Publications, 1987, ISBN 0 87773 642 1

Michael McMaster, *The Intelligence Advantage: Organising for Complexity*, Butterworth-Heinemann, 1996, ISBN 0 7506 9792 X

Marvin Weisbord and Sandra Janoff, *Future Search*, Berrett-Koehler, 1995, ISBN 1 881052 12 5

Complex Behaviour

"The chess-board is the world; the pieces are the phenomena of the universe; the rules of the game are what we call the Laws of Nature."

T.H. Huxley

'Complex behaviour' refers to the often paradoxical and surprising behaviour of simple-seeming systems governed by simple rules. In this section we examine the forces that operate to produce a kind of stability (what Onar Åm calls 'meta-balance') in complex systems. Computer simulation sits in the background of several of the entries in this section: computers are a key tool of complexity scientists. Several fondly held notions about change and change management are shown to be either erroneous or at best of limited use.

Complex Behaviour

Self-organisation
Complex behaviour need not have a complex explanation. Order will emerge from self-organisation. The way is open to a new and adaptive form of teamwork in which individuals manage themselves within clear boundaries.

The 'game of life'
The 'game of life' demonstrates the importance of iteration: making frequent small changes and observing the effects, rather than a 'big bang' approach. Global rules acting locally reveal the power of simplicity.

The 'edge of chaos'
Order isn't order, it's predictability and stereotypical behaviour. The 'edge of chaos' is present in all complex adaptive systems where it fosters learning and creativity.

Attractor
Attractors can be the basis of a new approach to organisational change. The concept of the attractor reminds us that there are organising principles at work in all systems. Values, goals, theories, leadership in groups: all can be considered as attractors bringing people together.

Increasing returns and lock-in

In complex adaptive systems, increasing returns are commonplace. The equilibrium mindset shuts out the possibilities offered by increasing returns. Lock-in to a less than optimal state is frequent: the market does not 'know best'.

Self-organisation

 ## Relevance

Complex behaviour need not have a complex explanation. Order will emerge from self-organisation. The way is open to a new and adaptive form of teamwork in which individuals manage themselves within clear boundaries.

Translation

Boids: a self-organised flock

Flocking is one version of what Kevin Kelly calls nature's favourite organisation design – the flock or swarm. Fish in schools, birds in flocks, bees and ants in swarms: co-ordinated masses of individual 'agents'. The 'boids' simulation is an incredibly simple and tiny computer program that successfully captures the essence of flocking behaviour, to such an extent that when shown to ornithologists they accused its creator, Craig Reynolds, of faking it by digitising film of birds in flight. The simulation is now accepted as a description of the actual mechanism that governs all flocking behaviour in organisms, after its successful empirical testing in the Galapagos.

Reynolds' basic idea was to place a large collection of autonomous, bird-like agents – 'boids' – into a computer-generated environment full of walls and obstacles. Each boid followed three simple rules of behaviour:

1. It tried to maintain a minimum distance from other objects in the environment, including other boids.

2. It tried to match velocities with boids in its neighbourhood.

3. It tried to move toward the perceived centre of mass of boids in its neighbourhood.

the 'game of life'

Notice that there is no rule that says 'form a flock'. Instead, as in the 'game of life', the rules were entirely 'local'; referring only to what an individual boid could 'see' and do in its own vicinity. So, if a flock forms, it forms from the 'bottom up' – there is no 'leader boid' telling all the others what to do in a 'top-down' hierarchical manner. As Nicholas Negroponte puts it: "The duck at the front is not the leader". When a flock forms, as it always does, it is an **emergent** network phenomenon.

It doesn't matter how the simulation is started off: it can start with the boids scattered around the computer screen completely at random and the rules will always 'force' the boids to form a flock. Look at it from the point of view of a single boid: if it is at the edge of the flock, rule 3 tells it to move in. If it is flying faster or slower than the boids near it, rule 2 says that it has to slow down or speed up. Rule 1 tells it to keep its distance from the others. (This distance, like the other rules, can be altered: different distances produce different types of flock reminiscent of different bird species.) So the boids spontaneously collect themselves into a flock that can fly around obstacles in a very fluid and natural manner, sometimes even breaking into 'sub-flocks' that flow around both sides of an obstacle, rejoining on the other side. In one of the runs, a boid 'accidentally' hit a pole, fluttered around for a moment as though dazed, and then flew on to rejoin the flock!

Three little rules for self-organisation
Reynolds feels that this 'dazed' boid proves that the overall behaviour of the boids is actually emergent. Nowhere in the rules does it say what the boid should do if it crashes into something. So part of the message is this: if we can explain something like flocking (that appears to be incredibly complicated) with three little rules, are there any other things that seem complicated that might turn out to be equally simple? The answer is Yes. This idea of emergent self-organisation has been successfully applied to explain the behaviour of traders

*increasing
returns and
lock-in*

in the stock market, and is generally applicable to any situation in which 'agents' are free to choose, without central control. We can hear this in the language of news reports: 'The market decided that the 3M flotation was overpriced' is a statement about the emergent behaviour arising from thousands of little transactions on the stock exchange; there was no-one actually telling them not to buy the 3M shares, nobody called a meeting.

Sensitivity to initial conditions

Initial conditions are often important in complexity theory. This is clearly illustrated in boids. In boids, it is all the other boids that largely determine what an individual boid will do. Think about releasing birds one at a time into a space: you could imagine that you have hundreds of pigeons in a net inside the Albert Hall, or some other vast building. When the first pigeon is released, its options are completely open; it can fly where it likes because the only rule that applies to it is rule 1: don't bump into anything, and the Albert Hall is huge. Release another pigeon and the options narrow dramatically: both birds now have to fly towards each other and match speeds in order to obey rules 2 and 3. The next one out of the net has no choices at all: it must head for the 'perceived centre of mass' (in between the first two birds) and match speed with them. What we have here is a robust phenomenon that is sensitive to initial conditions: a flock always forms, and the direction of flight is randomly determined by the results of the first few interactions.

Rules are tendencies

The rules aren't strict rules, they are perhaps better described as tendencies. Birds tend to fly together in flocks, they tend to move towards the centre of the flock. Natural selection has ensured that birds that didn't have this strong tendency were eaten by predators. So the rules make sense for the organisms most of the time; but if they weren't broken from time to time there would be no growth or change. It is in the nature of complex adaptive systems to push at the boundaries; species are always trying to expand out of their current niches: witness the fact that coyotes were found in the Bronx (reported in *The Observer*, 2 June 1996).

increasing returns and lock-in, ecosystem

'Critical mass': human flocking

'Critical mass' is an 'organised coincidence' which takes place in many cities. It started in San Francisco in 1994 and has spread across America and Europe. It is a once-a-month bike ride through major cities in the rush hour. The idea is to enjoy cycling in the city and to make a point about transport policy at the same time. Several hundred cyclists turn out and peacefully take over the streets for a couple of hours, just by riding *en masse*. All sorts of people are involved, from office workers to local government officers and transport campaign activists.

Critical mass is genuinely self-organised. Although it was started by a small group of cycling activists, they are not in charge of it and cannot control it. Someone will suggest a route and the group moves off in that direction. Once the 'flock' is moving, its direction is determined by the vagaries of other traffic, traffic signals and the mood of the people who happen to be at the front at the time. Just as in boids, a flock forms in a ragged organic way, under the pressure of the rules. In London traffic it is clear that not staying close to the other cyclists is dangerous: taxis and cars take the place of hawks, to establish rule 3: move toward

Self-organisation

the perceived centre of mass near you if you want to escape the cars. Rule 1 is just obvious: keep a minimum distance from other objects in the environment; as is rule 2: ride at the same speed as your neighbours. One UK participant commented:

> *"The pressure of the rules is amazing. I once got separated from the main group with about ten others – suddenly the traffic closed in, including cars whose drivers wanted to hold us personally responsible for delaying their journey home by a few minutes. The urge to rejoin the group as quickly as possible was incredible!"*

The emergence of the same three rules in a 'human system' is compelling evidence for the generality of the rules of self-organisation. Brian Eno speculates that there are three general classes of rules of which the boids rules are a particular case: a generative rule, a diminishing rule, and a maintenance rule.

 ## Application
What does 'boids' tell us?
Boids has two key messages: complex behaviour need not have a complex explanation, and order will emerge from 'self-organisation'. Management theorists develop complex explanations for behaviour in the workplace; it is often the case that a few underlying rules are 'powering' all the complex behaviour observed on the surface.

coevolution

The 'shifting the shift patterns' restaurant case study cited in the 'coevolution' entry in this book (p.190) can be viewed as an example of locked-in behaviour maintained by a few rules: the rules were changed and the behaviour changed.

The rules at work

In the restaurant case, the clue is that all the staff were sure that they would suffer personally, although they could see the benefits of the proposed change. This is a clue to the interdependency that boids-type rules generate. The environment for the birds in the simulation is mainly made up of other birds. In a restaurant, the actions of the workers are similarly strongly interdependent. If one waiter doesn't turn up for work, all the waiting staff suffer. When tips are pooled, a peer-pressure rule ensures that everyone pulls their weight. So we can describe the interactions of the staff as taking place on a fitness landscape in which the shape of the landscape is mainly determined by the actions of the other staff. They are their own environment (this idea has echoes of the self-referentiality of autopoiesis). When the rules were changed by their manager introducing the new shift pattern, they all changed their behaviour together, like a flock.

autopoiesis

A new view of team leadership

attractor

The illusion of co-ordination which emerges in boids can also be viewed as an 'attractor'. Where is the leadership in the leaderless flock? Leadership is the emergent behaviour of the whole system. Is this perhaps what is going on in teams? How often do we assume that there must be a leader? As Michael McMaster says: "Try viewing leadership as an attractor." In the restaurant example, their manager is also one of the team; she is not leading in the sense of telling people what to do from minute to minute. Her role as manager is to set the rules to create the appropriate emergence. This is the true meaning of self-organisation. Like many scientific terms it can be misleading, a clearer though more unwieldy term would be 'rule-driven self-organisation'.

dialogue

Self-organisation points the way to a new, more open and adaptable form of teamwork in which individuals manage themselves within clear boundaries.

Cross-references

attractor, evolution of co-operation, coevolution, increasing returns and lock-in

References

Brian Eno, *A Year with Swollen Appendices: Brian Eno's Diary*, Faber and Faber, 1996, ISBN 0 571 17995 9

Kevin Kelly, *Out of Control: the New Biology of Machines*, Fourth Estate, 1994, ISBN 1 85702 308 0

Nicholas Negroponte, *Being Digital*, Coronet Books, 1995, ISBN 0 34064 930 5

M. Mitchell Waldrop, *Complexity: the Emerging Science at the Edge of Order and Chaos*, Penguin, 1994, ISBN 0 140 179 682

 Relevance

The 'game of life' demonstrates the importance of iteration: making frequent small changes and observing the effects, rather than a 'big bang' approach. Global rules acting locally reveal the power of simplicity.

Translation

The 'game of life' is an example of a cellular automaton: a type of computer program invented in the mid-1950s by John von Neumann to study 'self-replication'. Because cellular automata are self-replicating, they share some of the features of life itself. Computer simulation is used extensively in complexity research: it makes a new sort of scientific enquiry possible answering 'What if?' questions with repeated iterations to explore all the possibilities of a situation. The 'game of life' was invented by John Conway in the mid 70s: it is a drastically simplified version of von Neumann's cellular automaton having only two rules. It represents 'live' cells as black squares on a grid of white squares: the grid can be any size and each cell has two states:

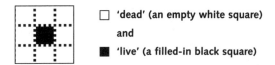

☐ 'dead' (an empty white square)

and

■ 'live' (a filled-in black square)

The state of every cell on the board changes from one 'generation' to the next, according to the states of its eight nearest neighbours.

The rules of the simulation: 'Life' rules

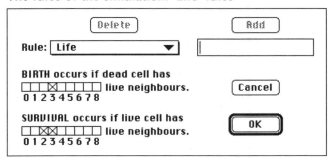

The 'rules of life' state that:

- a dead square becomes alive IF it has exactly three live neighbours
- a live cell dies out IF it has less than two or more than three live neighbours.

Think global, act local
The 'game of life' simply involves starting off with any pattern of live cells and seeing what happens. Strange complex patterns seem to 'boil' across the screen of the computer, reminiscent of plant growth speeded up, or the movement of flocks of birds or a crowd.

Each time the game 'iterates' (the mathematician's word for a 'turn' in a game) a new generation is born from the old one. The fate of a square on the board is determined with reference only to the state of its neighbours, and this applies to each of its neighbours as well, and so on, for every square on the board. The rules apply to every square equally: **global** rules interpreted **locally**.

The 'game of life' demonstrates emergence, replication and unpredictability. Because of this, it offers provocative insights into the nature of all complex systems, including living things and human organisations. Even though the rules are completely deterministic, it is **impossible** to predict whether an arbitrary starting pattern will die out, or start oscillating, or fill the grid. Thus cellular automata provide a powerful demonstration of how an incredibly simple system can generate extremely complex behaviour. (A written description cannot really do justice to the results: the solution is to obtain a copy to run on your computer. See below for details.)

The 'game of life'

Patterns and rules

There are four general concepts here, which can be applied to a vast range of situations. They are:

- starting pattern
- global rules applying to everything in the 'game' but with
- local interpretation producing a local effect
- initial conditions – the combination of the starting pattern and the rules.

self-organisation

Any pattern will change as rules are applied to it by the game: the patterns illustrated here tend to occur often in the program. Under the 'life' rules these patterns, (which we can call 'flower', 'bead', 'cross', 'bar', 'diagonal bar', 'square', 'dot', and 'glider'), quickly settle down into static or oscillating states. (The 'glider' is a special kind of oscillator, so-called because it also moves across the board as it oscillates.)

Some common patterns in the 'game of life'

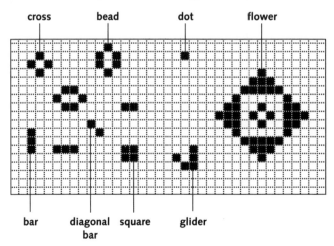

The 'game of life'

Another fascinating pattern is the one that produces the so-called 'glider gun'.

The start position of the 'glider gun'

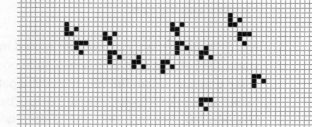

Like all the patterns in the 'game of life', the 'glider gun' was discovered by patient examination of huge numbers of initial starting patterns. Because these patterns **emerge**, it is simply not possible to determine the outcome of a pattern any other way. Thirteen gliders come together and form the two-part 'glider gun' which then merrily pumps out gliders which fly off to the south-east for ever and ever (or until another pattern on the board interacts with them).

The 'glider gun'

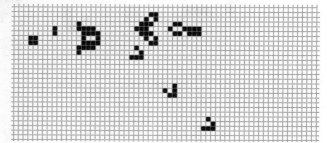

The emergence of this pattern from random patterns is uncannily reminiscent of the emergence of life, and demonstrates Kauffman's contention that order arises spontaneously even in quite simple systems. Participants at 'Navigating Complexity' workshops were fascinated by it, comparing it to a small department in a business quietly working away: processing requisitions or customer orders.

Changing the rules

As can be seen from the following, the impact of different rules on the same starting patterns is dramatic. The same basic patterns are shown iterated according to different sets of rules: the 'game of life' rules and the 'lacy' rules. (They are called 'lacy' rules because of the type of pattern they typically produce.)

The 'game of life' rules:
- a dead square becomes alive IF it has EXACTLY three live neighbours
- a live cell survives IF it has two OR three live neighbours.

The 'lacy' rules:
- a dead square becomes alive IF it has one OR three live neighbours
- a live cell survives IF it has two OR three live neighbours.

Life rules	Lacy rules

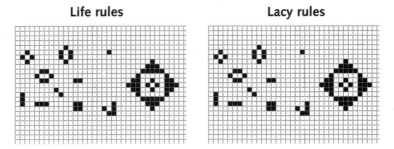

Iteration: 0

Life rules   ## Lacy rules

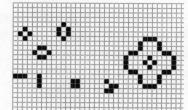 

Iteration: 1

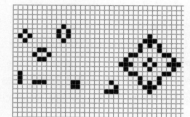 

Iteration: 2

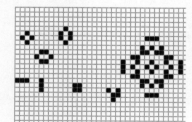 

Iteration: 3

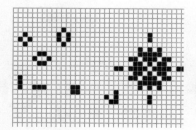 

Iteration: 4

The 'game of life'

Notation for rules: different sets of rules are recorded using a special notation. The notation for 'life' rules is as follows: 'B3 S23', which means birth if 3, survival if 2 or 3. The 'Lacy' rules differ only in one respect; the birth rule is 1 or 3 neighbours, represented as: 'B13, S23'. There are obviously lots of other possible combinations of rules.

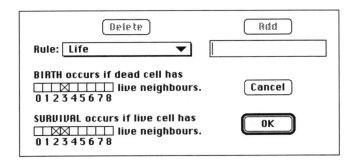

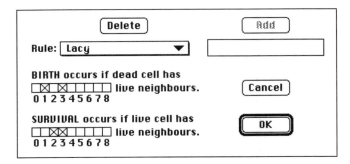

Although they differ only slightly from the 'life' rules, the 'lacy' rules quickly cause the separate cells to merge together into a mass which grows larger with each iteration. Workshop participants compared the lacy pattern to a city or a castle, because it seemed to have walls and some internal structure, as well as openings to the 'outside' (see iteration 3 above). Some participants felt that the oscillating forms (the bars and crosses) represented rigid bureaucracies which were now 'just going through the motions' without reference to the outside world.

Application
Set it up, then iterate

There are many implications to be drawn from the 'game of life'. It offers a large number of metaphors and images which can stimulate new thinking and learning. It underlines the importance of getting the right conditions at the start of a project, at the same time reminding us that the resulting behaviour may not be what was expected. It also seems to be saying that if managers 'free up' a situation and allow staff some leeway in interpreting the rules, then greater creativity can result, without falling over into chaos. It stresses the importance of iteration; making frequent small changes rather than a 'big bang' approach.

self-organisation, evolution of co-operation

Rules in organisations

A universally applicable voluntary redundancy package in an organisation seems reminiscent of a global rule. The effects of the rule would depend both on the other rules operating in the organisation and the actions of individual players in response to those rules. The way that individuals decide whether to accept the package or not is definitely a 'local' interpretation. Much as we might wish otherwise, the individual decides what is best for themselves, not what is best for the employer.

Cross-references
evolution of co-operation, the 'edge of chaos', self-organisation

The 'game of life'

References

Jack Cohen and Ian Stewart, *The Collapse of Chaos: Discovering Simplicity in a Complex World*, Penguin, 1995, ISBN 0 14 0178 740

David Peak and Michael Frame, *Chaos under Control: the Art and Science of Complexity*, New York, Freeman and Co., 1994, ISBN 0716 724 294 (see chapter 9)

Lifelab is the freeware version of the 'game of life' for the Macintosh computer, from which the 'screenshots' shown here are taken (used with thanks). Artificial life software is widely available on the Internet and the World Wide Web in versions for MS-DOS, Windows, Macintosh and Unix systems. Some is commercial software; most of it is shareware or freeware. The LGMB Organisational Learning project has a website with further details at:
http://www.netsquared.com/LGMB-complex

The 'edge of chaos'

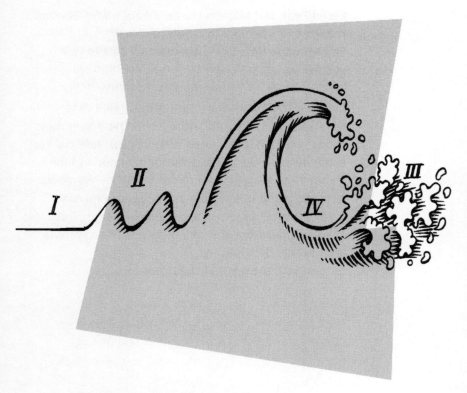

 Relevance
Order isn't order, it's predictability and stereotypical behaviour. The 'edge of chaos' is present in all complex adaptive systems where it fosters learning and creativity.

Translation

The 'edge of chaos': where order makes the transition to complexity

Don't be misled by the word 'chaos': this 'edge of chaos' is a technical term that should not be viewed pejoratively; it has little in common with the chaos advocated by 80s management gurus like Tom Peters. It is a term describing the point in a complex system when ordered behaviour gives way to turbulent behaviour: 'a phase transition' such as the change from ice to water or water to steam. This phase transition is an example of one of four classes of behaviour which occur time and time again in complexity science. Three of them were discovered in research into non-linear dynamical systems: systems which exhibit 'chaotic' behaviour. These are:

- Class I   Stasis

- Class II   Order

- Class III   Chaos

network and hierarchy, the 'game of life'

The fourth – the 'edge of chaos' – was discovered later by several of the founders of complexity theory, working independently, including Stuart Kauffman, who studies Boolean NK networks, and Chris Langton, who studies cellular automata such as the 'game of life'. The fourth class of behaviour is:

- Class IV   Complexity

Class IV appears in between II and III. This is because complexity exists on the 'edge of chaos', poised between order and chaos. Langton argues that:

"You should look at systems in terms of how they behave, instead of how they're made. When you do, what you find are the two extremes of order and chaos. In between the two extremes, at a kind of abstract phase transition called the 'edge of chaos', you also find complexity: a class of behaviours in which the components of the system never quite lock into place, yet never quite dissolve into turbulence either. These are the systems that are both stable enough to store information, and yet evanescent enough to transmit. These are the systems that can be organised to perform complex computation, to react to the world, to be spontaneous, adaptive, and alive."

The 'edge of chaos' isn't an edge, it's a zone

These four classes can be represented by analogy in the diagram opposite. Note that the 'edge of chaos' isn't actually an edge: as Langton says, it is a class of behaviours. As an orderly system starts to break down, like the wave patterns in the diagram, the breakdowns happen more and more frequently until the system is completely chaotic. In surfing, the area under the about-to-break wave is known as the 'tube': surfers attempt to ride the tube, just ahead of the point where the tube breaks as the wave hits the beach. In this analogy, this is the zone of complexity, the zone in which possibilities open up.

possibility space

We can also show the four classes in a Venn diagram: this is useful if we want to discuss moving from one zone to another. IBM is used by Michael McMaster as an example of the typical journey of a company from the 'edge of chaos', as a small 'start-up', slipping back into predictable ordered behaviour as it grows larger. In the diagram the dotted lines link the wave diagram to the equivalent parts of the Venn diagram.

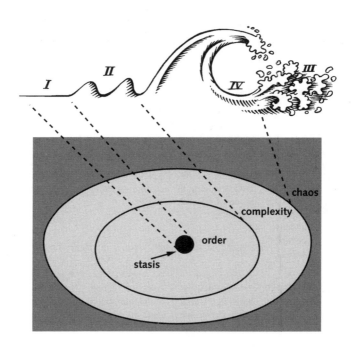

Order isn't order, it's predictability and stereotypical behaviour

All living systems operate in the zone of complexity. This doesn't mean that it is a comfortable place to be – it's not. In human systems, the automatic tendency is to avoid the onset of 'chaos' whenever possible. But it's also important to avoid 'order' whenever possible; the place to be is the zone of complexity, the 'edge of chaos'. Let's be clear about this term 'order'. In this context, it doesn't mean a well-oiled machine, smoothly ticking over. Like the 'edge of chaos' it is a technical term. When applied to human systems, it translates as predictability and stereotypical behaviour. An ordered organisation is one that is not adapting, not responding to change, just 'going through the motions' – repeating a set of patterns of response over and over again, complacent and unresponsive.

the 'game of life'

The table below describes the four classes in relation to the 'game of life', information state, organisation analogy, and Langton's λ (Lambda) factor.

Class	'Game of life' pattern state	Information state	λ*	Organisation analogy
Class I STASIS	Unchanging patterns of cells	Information cannot be transmitted	0	A defunct organisation
Class II ORDER (Stability, equilibrium, stereotypical patterns)	Cells oscillating between a set of two or more states, in an eventually repeating pattern	Some information passes between cells, similar to crystal growth	0.01- 0.279	Large corporations like IBM in the early 80s, complacent and unresponsive, going through the motions – repeating a set of patterns over and over again
Class IV COMPLEXITY	Complex patterns of live cells, displaying elements of order and elements of disorder; evolving, changing patterns	Information can be transmitted; enough flexibility to transmit messages, enough stability to support a message structure	0.28	An effective creative team, small company start-ups like Apple and Microsoft in the late 70s
Class III CHAOS	Cells grow and die chaotically with no discernible pattern	Information cannot be transmitted: no stability to support a message structure, no flexibility to transmit messages	0.5	A department at war with itself: no useful work is done, endless meetings and discussions, etc.

*As λ increases, the cycle time of repeating patterns gets longer and longer. Applied to the 'game of life', λ is the probability that any cell will be alive on the next iteration: thus a λ of 0.5 represents random chance.

The 'edge of chaos' is present in all complex adaptive systems

complex adaptive systems

Complex adaptive systems which include ecosystems, the economy, animals and human beings and which exist in groups like hives, swarms or flocks, or societies and organisations, all display the same emergent patterns of creative, adaptive behaviour. They are exquisitely tuned to their environment, learning from

The 'edge of chaos'

it, responding to it, changing it in the process and being changed by it.

autopoiesis

All complex adaptive systems are also autopoietic systems. The constant tension between order and chaos that we call complexity can be seen as the result of two constantly interacting dynamic processes:

- **the autopoietic urge** to maintain identity, to constantly re-create the self, to resist change, and to focus inwards
- **the vital urge** of all living things to change, to grow, to explore to the limit, and to focus outwards.

These two tendencies are represented in the diagrams below:

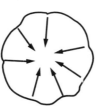 

autopoietic urge   **vital urge**

Application
The 'edge of chaos' in human experience: flow

Mihaly Csikszentmihalyi has spent more than two decades researching the 'psychology of happiness'. His main findings are summed up in his bestseller *Flow*. He describes 'flow' as the feeling that everything is going just right, be it an interesting conversation, a piece of work, a game of tennis or an improvised solo in jazz. The 'edge of chaos' can be felt clearly in many 'flow' activities: the mountain biker's perfect downhill, never quite falling off, not daring to control the descent by braking because that will definitely cause a crash; or the surfer surfing a perfect wave just ahead of it breaking onto the beach. Flow happens at work as well: in fact, Csikszentmihalyi says that most people tend to experience flow far more at work than in their leisure time slumped in front of the TV. At work, flow can happen in one of those deep conversations where the insights and the difficulties are mixed together as the talkers learn from each other at the limits of their understanding, or simply working in the sort of office where it always feels like things are going to collapse any minute but they never do. Unfortunately in many situations the slight 'loosening' that could enable creativity to blossom is not enabled because of management's fear of a collapse into chaos.

possibility space

Learning and creativity at the 'edge of chaos'
The possibility space, or zone of possibility as Michael McMaster calls it, expands massively at the 'edge of chaos'. This space or zone is a metaphor for the place where creative ideas come into being in individuals or groups. Creativity can only happen if individuals are free to operate at their own 'edge of chaos'. These ideas have been explored by Sheila Harri-Augstein who developed the concept of 'self-organised learning' (SOL). SOL is based on the idea that the individual is the expert in their own learning, and should therefore be supported rather than taught. The point at which our learning almost breaks down is seen as the point of real creativity and rich learning in SOL.

The methods of SOL are now applied in companies and universities worldwide.

The 'edge of chaos'

"Learning operates on the edge of chaos, somewhere between a stable system of order and an unstable system of disorder! It is here that personal meaning, a person's system of personal knowing, gets constructed. At the two extremes of the behaviour of all systems, **order** *and* **chaos** *pervades. Between these two extremes, at the edge of chaos, one finds complexity! This is a class of behaviours in which the components of the system are neither stable, nor in a state of randomness. Complexity is now recognised as the state that allows information to organise and reorganise itself to increasing degrees of sophistication. This is the state that allows the person to construct new and more complex meanings."*

Sheila Harri-Augstein on the 'edge of chaos'

Please note the unfortunate confusion here between individually organised and controlled learning (which Harri-Augstein calls 'self-organised learning') and the central complexity idea of 'self-organising' behaviour in groups of agents. The two are closely related, but not identical. In 'self-organised learning', the self-organising is taking place **inside** the learner's brain (which is a complex adaptive system in its own right) rather than in a networked group of individuals. Both ideas are examples of a broad set of approaches to adult education sometimes called 'student-centred' or 'learner-centred' approaches. To add to the confusion (for the sake of completeness) there is yet another similar approach, known as 'self-managed learning'.

self-organisation, complex adaptive systems

"Learning is about our personal voyage of deep inner-self-discovery. It cannot be reduced to blindly following rules set up by others. It involves challenging automatic, robotic behaviour and being demanding as a learner both of others and ourselves. Self-organised learning is a lifetime's work with tremendous personal pay-offs. Without learning we remain static and unchanged."

Sheila Harri-Augstein on 'self-organised learning'

Phase transitions in groups

Ralph Stacey explores the idea of adaptive feedback networks, and how organisations can create space for creativity, in his book *Complexity and Creativity in Organisations*. He develops the idea of the 'phase transition' as a creator of space for novelty and learning in groups and teams,

The 'edge of chaos'

linking psychoanalytic ideas with learning theory and complexity theory.

It can be very fruitful to apply the idea of phase transitions to work with groups, in a similar way to that described by Harri-Augstein in the individual learner. The strategy is to judge where the group is in relation to the 'edge of chaos', then take only those actions that will efficiently move the group toward the edge. This is very different from conventional groupwork practice.

Applying the 'edge of chaos' concept

The 'edge' is a very powerful metaphor. The edge is the point at which a system interacts with its environment; the point at which the system is at risk, vulnerable to change or collapse, but also open to learning. The edge could be:

- the edge of the whole organisation, the edge of a unit or department, or the edge of a team
- the edge of ideas
- the edge of learning
- the edge of acceptability of proposals
- the edge in permaculture, where food production is greatest.

ecosystem/ permaculture

The edge is clearly a risky place to be: but can any organisation afford not to spend some time there? Playing safe is not a viable option in the face of massive change and unpredictability.

The edge concept can be applied to any situation where learning, dialogue, information transmission, creativity, or possibility are needed.

The 'edge of chaos'

Cross-references

the 'game of life', network and hierarchy, complex adaptive systems, complexity

References

Mihaly Csikszentmihalyi, *Flow: the Psychology of Happiness*, Rider, 1992, ISBN 0 7126 5477 1

Sheila Harri-Augstein and Ian M.Webb, *Learning to Change*, McGraw-Hill, 1995, ISBN 0 07 707896 9

Michael McMaster, *The Intelligence Advantage: Organising for Complexity*, Butterworth-Heinemann, 1996, ISBN 0 7506 9792 X

Ralph Stacey, *Complexity and Creativity in Organisations*, Berrett-Koehler, 1996, ISBN 1 881052 89 3

M. Mitchell Waldrop, *Complexity: the Emerging Science at the Edge of Order and Chaos*, Penguin, 1994, ISBN 0 140 179 682

Attractor

 Relevance

Attractors can be the basis of a new approach to organisational change. The concept of the attractor reminds us that there are organising principles at work in all systems. Values, goals, theories, leadership in groups: all can be considered as attractors bringing people together.

Translation

What is an attractor?

An attractor is a model representation of the behavioural results of a system. The attractor is not a force of attraction or a goal-oriented presence in the system, but simply depicts where the system is heading, based on the rules of motion in the system. In other words, it is more like the drifting of a boat in a slow current in a wide river than a magnet pulling iron filings towards itself. The concept of the attractor comes from chaos theory (which is now part of complexity science). It is a complex mathematical concept which explains the behaviour of 'dynamical' systems using the idea of 'phase space' – an imaginary mathematical space which represents all the possibilities in a situation. The interested reader is directed to Cohen and Stewart's book, *The Collapse of Chaos*, for a full explanation of these ideas. In the pages that follow three sorts of attractor are described:

The term 'attractor' is descriptive, but the word seems to imply a prescriptive force. In the context of management, one more word must be added – 'passive'. The attractor just is – it is a passive state not an active force. The passivity of an attractor means that the 'actors' moving with it can drift from one attractor to another. Thanks to Michael Lissack for highlighting this important distinction.

- the point attractor
- the closed loop attractor
- the strange attractor.

The ice-cream attractor

Cohen and Stewart point out that if there are two ice-cream men working a mile-long stretch of beach (between the cliff and the pier, say) then logically they should place themselves an equal distance apart, in the positions shown in the following diagram. (If the distance between the cliff and the pier is x, their positions should be a $1/4 \, x$ from the cliff or pier and a $1/2 \, x$ apart.)

That way nobody has to walk further than a quarter of a mile to get an ice-cream. But this **never** happens. Both of the sellers will be found at the same spot in the middle of the stretch of beach. Why? Because of an attractor. If the first seller edges a tiny bit closer to the other one, they can steal a few customers from the other. Equally if the other seller edges a tiny bit closer to the first one, they can also steal a few customers. So inevitably they both end up almost on top of each other in the middle of the beach, and most people have to walk twice as far to get an ice-cream. (Cohen and Stewart use this as an example of the failed idea that 'free market forces automatically produce the best result' – an idea further explored by Brian Arthur and Paul Ormerod in the notion of 'lock-in'.) The centre of the beach is an attractor for ice-cream sellers: it is the point in phase space that sucks them in. This is the basic idea of the attractor.

increasing returns and lock-in

Attractors in the UK
Many towns owe their existence to an attractor: towns which grew up at a convenient crossing point on a river like Exeter and Cambridge, or towns which grew massively during the industrial revolution like Birmingham and Middlesbrough. In each case, a set of favourable initial conditions led to a massive increase in growth.

self-organisation

More complex attractors

The ice-cream seller attractor is a simple 'point' attractor; an attractor can be much more complex than this. The relationship between predator and prey is an example of a 'closed loop' attractor: as the number of rabbits increases, the number of foxes increases, and vice versa. The loop describes the various positions in phase space of the numbers of animals. It is a loop because the two species are linked together, rising and falling in number as the other species rises and falls, locked into the cycle. In the diagram on the left below, several loops are shown; each loop represents a different set of initial conditions (number of rabbits, number of foxes). There are actually an infinite number of possible loops, but only four are shown for clarity.

The relationship of fox and rabbit populations as attractor

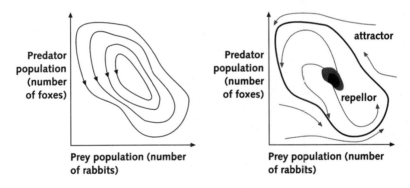

Predator population (number of foxes)

Prey population (number of rabbits)

Predator population (number of foxes)

attractor

repellor

Prey population (number of rabbits)

Strictly speaking, this diagram is too simplistic. The one on the right is a better model: it has only one closed loop. All other cycles will spiral towards it, except for the point in its centre. The closed loop represents a stable dynamic state: an attractor. The point is a repellor, an unstable dynamic state. When a dynamic system is in a place in-between the point and the loop, it will be 'pushed' out to the loop. The arrows represent the effect of the attractor 'pulling' systems towards it, and the repellor pushing them away.

Strange attractors

Fundamentally unpredictable attractors are known as 'strange attractors'; they explain why tiny divergences in complex systems like the weather can cause huge changes. We can compare two points on a strange attractor in phase space to two people on two trains stopped in a station talking to each other through the open windows of the carriage. The moment the trains pull out, heading for different destinations on two different tracks, the two trains will rapidly move far apart, never to meet again. This analogy also emphasises the idea of sensitivity to initial conditions: get on the wrong train and you end up somewhere completely different.

self-organisation, the 'game of life'

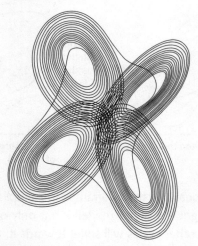

The Lorentz attractor: an example of a strange attractor

Certain types of differential equation produce strange attractors which can be represented graphically. Successive iterations produce the complex plot shown; the curve looping round and round on one of the loops, then moving over to the other side and looping round before moving on again, and so on...

Reaching a peak of fitness in a basin

The term 'basin of attraction' is often used to depict the idea that systems drift down into the attractor state from their initial position.

In the 'ice-cream attractor' described above, once the two ice-cream sellers are at the midpoint, they are stuck at the bottom of the 'basin of attraction'. Unless the rules change in some way they won't be able to get out: they are 'locked-in'.

increasing returns and lock-in

The idea of the attractor has strongly influenced the concept of 'lock-in'

fitness landscape

We can literally turn the idea of the 'basin of attraction' on its head to give us the idea of a 'fitness peak'. Another way of describing the final state of the two ice-cream sellers is as a 'local fitness peak'. It is the place to which they have evolved, where they are well fitted to their environment; it is a hilltop in the fitness landscape.

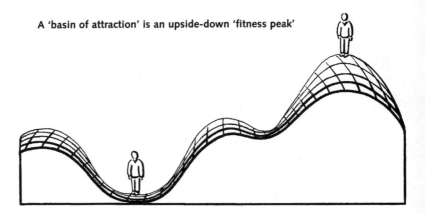

A 'basin of attraction' is an upside-down 'fitness peak'

Like the monkey with its hand in the jar of peanuts, who can't escape because he won't let go of the nuts so that he can pull his hand out of the narrow neck of the jar, the ice-cream sellers are stuck in the basin of attraction. It is the 'best' place for them to be, given their refusal to co-operate with each other. They are stuck there because to move from that point would mean an immediate reduction in profits, which has to be set against a future **possible** increase in profits. Similarly, in the fitness landscape, they cannot leave their local hilltop to migrate to another higher hill, much as they might want to, because they have evolved to sell ice-cream as sole traders and have reached their peak of competence in their trade. They can't easily change, anymore than cheetahs can switch to eating grass if they run out of gazelles.

coevolution

Application
Attractor as metaphor
The attractor is a powerful metaphor which can assist new thinking in 'possibility space' (the metaphorical equivalent of phase space). For example, memes are linguistic attractors. In a group discussion, an idea can 'derail' the group, locking it into a discussion which can wander far away from the original topic. Equally, other ideas can act as benign attractors, 'pulling together' other ideas.

metaphor, possibility space, memes

'Field of Dreams': attractors at work
Hollywood provides one of the best illustrations of attractors at work in a community. In the Kevin Costner movie 'Field of Dreams', a young farmer risks financial ruin and builds the baseball pitch that he sees in his recurring dream. 'If you build it, they will come' the voices tell him, and they do. One by one a dream

team of very solid looking ghosts from baseball's past appear on the pitch that he has created in the middle of his cornfield. Paying spectators also arrive, ensuring that he doesn't lose his farm in the process. The film is an extended metaphor for optimism and the power of the self-fulfilling prophecy. If we also view it as a metaphor for leadership, it can offer us some new insights.

Commitment and leadership as an attractor
Michael McMaster suggests that ideas like leadership and commitment are dangerously misleading. He prefers to apply the idea of the attractor to describe the process by which a project starts to take off.

> "Consider the idea that once a group, team or project has started, it has a force of its own that is either strong enough to continue or will die. The thing that we call individual commitment will occur naturally if certain conditions are present and will not if they are not. What are these conditions? What needs to occur for commitment to occur in a team?

> Complexity theory suggests that the energy and information available will flow towards and around 'attractors'. These attractors will create positive returns, that is, they will continue and even build on their own if they are sufficiently strong and function within the system. The attractors may be values, principles, goals, theories, emotion – many things. We can probably only focus on a few of them.

> There is another very important attractor that has been neglected because it has been made into a matter of personality, psychology and authority. That is, someone

with a clear intention, a great deal of energy, etc., is an
attractor. In this sense, a project can certainly use a leader
to continue successfully. Once the leader (or team) has
been effective at replacing the leader in individual form
with strong attractors which are independent of the leader,
then the team can be expected to continue on its own. It's
not a matter of 'commitment'. It's much less personal and
individual than that – given this model. Try viewing
leadership as 'being an attractor' and see what it gives
you."

Michael McMaster in a posting to the Learning Organisation
email discussion group

 ## Cross-references
increasing returns and lock-in, possibility space,
memes, fitness landscape, coevolution

 ## References

Jack Cohen and Ian Stewart, *The Collapse of Chaos:*
Discovering Simplicity in a Complex World, Penguin,
1995, ISBN 0 14 0178 740

Michael McMaster, *The Intelligence Advantage:*
Organising for Complexity, Butterworth-Heinemann,
1996, ISBN 0 7506 9792 X

M. Mitchell Waldrop, *Complexity: the Emerging*
Science at the Edge of Order and Chaos, Penguin,
1994, ISBN 0 140 179 682

Increasing returns
and lock-in

 Relevance

In complex adaptive systems, increasing returns are commonplace. The equilibrium mindset shuts out the possibilities offered by increasing returns. Lock-in to a less than optimal state is frequent: the market does not 'know best'.

Translation

"Once random economic events select a particular path, the choice may become locked in regardless of the advantage of the alternative. [...]Cultivate increasing returns. Each time you use an idea, a language, or a skill you strengthen it, reinforce it, and make it more likely to be used again. That's known as positive feedback or snowballing. Success breeds success. The law operates in economics, biology, computer science, and human psychology. Life on earth alters earth to beget more life. Confidence builds confidence. Order generates more order. Them that has, gets. "

Kevin Kelly

Increasing returns is positive feedback

'Heavy metal' music provides a familiar example of positive feedback: the guitarist standing legs splayed wide, long hair flailing about, introduces his instrument to one of the loudspeakers on stage; an extremely loud distorted howl starts up, building louder and louder: the guitarist can 'play' the feedback by moving the guitar closer or further away from the speaker to produce effects which are considered musical by some. If the guitar is left in front of the speaker the sound will get louder and louder until it blows up the amplifiers and speakers. This is why positive feedback is commonly seen as the rogue relation of negative feedback, despite the great benefits that Kevin Kelly refers to above.

In tests, eight out of ten engineers preferred negative feedback

Ask an engineer to design a system of any kind and they will design it to include some form of negative feedback, in order to protect both the mechanism and the user. Nearly all machines are made this way. A good example is a domestic central heating system which uses a boiler linked to radiators to make the rooms warmer. But if the boiler stays on, the temperature will continue to rise and rise as the boiler gets hotter and hotter and eventually it will blow itself up. That's why boilers are fitted with a thermostat to control the temperature: when the thermostat detects that the room temperature has reached the setting, it signals to the boiler to turn itself off. The temperature then starts to fall and sometime later the thermostat will tell the boiler to come on again. The room will then start to warm up again and the thermostat will tell the boiler to shut off again and so on. This circular activity which 'manages' the boiler is known as a negative feedback loop. The underlying concept in negative feedback is that of equilibrium: balance or stability. But notice that our heating system never actually reaches equilibrium; it is always above or below the set temperature.

Life is increasing returns

The positive feedback loop is everywhere in nature: rabbit populations 'explode' in areas where foxes have been hunted to extinction; every new generation massively increasing the numbers of offspring in the next one. Life itself is a series of increasing returns: plants bind the sun's energy to make something from nothing, which feeds animals, which reproduce and so on and so on. Species constantly 'push their luck' constantly moving outwards, moving into habitats where their chances of survival are slender. Recently coyotes, wild turkey and deer were found in the Bronx... Any organism that isn't 'increasing its returns' is losing out. 'Running to stay still' is the order of the day.

Increasing returns in economics: lock-in

Despite the ubiquity of increasing returns in the real world, neo-classical economics is still mainly concerned with decreasing returns. Brian Arthur, of the Santa Fé Institute, has pointed out that many phenomena in economics do not conform to the Newtonian ideas of equilibrium and the single solution. He has worked with Stuart Kauffman, also at the SFI, applying Kauffman's work on Boolean NK networks to the problems of technological change in the economy. Technology evolves in a way very similar to ecosystems: new products, such as the laser printer, open up new niches for many other products such as desk-top publishing and graphics programs. The more the new technologies interconnect, the more they become locked-in. He offers a number of other examples of this 'lock-in'.

network and hierarchy, ecosystem

'Qwerty' typewriter keyboards The familiar 'Qwerty' layout of the typewriter was originally developed (in 1873) to make it harder to type, because typists kept jamming the keys by typing too quickly on early mechanical typewriters. Despite this obvious drawback, 'Qwerty' remains the dominant layout, although other, easier to learn and faster alternatives exist, such as the Dvorak layout.

Clockwise The format of our clocks is the result of historical accident. There is a Paolo Uccello clock on Florence Cathedral, designed in 1443, which has hands which move 'counter-clockwise' around a 24 hour dial. After 1550, 'clockwise' (12 hour) designs crowded out other designs.

VHS videocassettes When launched, the VHS format was inferior to Betamax. But, because more films were available on VHS, the early sales were of VHS rather than Betamax video recorders. As more sold, more people wanted to buy them: increasing returns.

Microsoft Windows and MS-DOS on desktop PCs
The initial take-up of MS-DOS is due to what has been described as the 'biggest single business strategy error ever', when IBM decided to license rather than own the MS-DOS operating system designed for their personal computers. This gave Microsoft a crucial advantage which they exploited to the full to convert DOS users to Windows, using a strategy that Brian Arthur describes as "target, leverage, link and lock". "You could say that Microsoft is the product of clever strategy, mediocre technology and a hell of a lot of increasing returns." (Brian Arthur quoted in 'Mine, All Mine', *Time*, 5 June 1995.)

> *"Increasing-returns economics has strong parallels with modern non-linear physics. [...] The parts of the economy that are resource-based (agriculture, bulk-goods productions, mining) are still, for the most part, subject to diminishing returns. Here conventional economics rightly holds sway. The parts of the market that are knowledge-based, on the other hand, are solely subject to increasing returns. Products such as computers, pharmaceuticals, missiles, aircraft, automobiles, software, telecommunications equipment or fibre optics are complicated to design and to manufacture. They require large initial investments in research, development and tooling, but once sales begin, incremental production is relatively cheap."*
>
> Brian Arthur

It's obvious (except to economists)
Although some economists have long recognised that increasing returns do occur in the economy, before Brian Arthur they had no theory to explain them. As John Darwin, ex-head of economic development at Sheffield, points out:

"...many of the phenomena most obvious to those practising economic development are manifest examples of increasing returns. One or two firms in a new industry choose a location, and this influences others to do the same, leading to a process of concentration through positive feedback and self-reinforcement. The relative success of the economies of Baden-Wurttemberg, Silicon Valley, Route 128 and the M4 corridor are all examples of the creation of self-reinforcing critical mass through positive returns."

John Holland has created an 'artificial stock exchange' with Brian Arthur and the physicist Richard Palmer, based on suggestions from discussions with the Nobel laureates Kenneth Arrow (economics) and Philip Anderson (physics). In this electronic arena, mindless but greedy automata bid against one another's strategies, giving rise to speculative bubbles, crashes and other real-life phenomena that classical economics has difficulty reproducing.

Positive feedback economics
Mitchell Waldrop provides a useful summary of the characteristics of Brian Arthur's approach to economics:

Increasing returns and lock-in

Neo-classical (conventional economics)	Positive feedback economics
Dominant assumption of decreasing returns in theories	Acknowledgement and study of increasing returns
Determinism, predictability, equilibrium, balance: ideas drawn from 19th century physics	Structure, pattern, self-organisation, life cycle: ideas drawn from biology
Assumes that people are identical	Assumes that people are different and are 'independent agents'
There is a single end-point of balance which can be reached	External effects and differences are key drivers. Any economic system is constantly 'unfolding': there is no end-point
Elements are quantities and prices	Elements are patterns and possibilities
No real dynamics in the sense that everything is at equilibrium	Economy is constantly on the edge of time. It rushes forward, structures constantly coalescing, decaying, changing
History is unimportant	History is crucial
'The market knows best'	Lock-ins produce inefficiency in the market
Structurally simple	Inherently complex
Economics as soft physics	Economics as high complexity science

(adapted from Waldrop)

Official: the market does not know best (the Qwerty effect)

'Post-orthodox economist', Paul Ormerod, points out that the assumption of increasing returns means that the market does not automatically 'know best'. The better product can win, but so can its inferior rival, as demonstrated by the outcome of the battle between Apple Computer with its Macintosh operating system, and Microsoft with MS-DOS and Windows.

> *"In short, the economics of 'Qwerty' (positive feedback) provides a general model for market failure, for how market forces can lock the economy into an inefficient path from which it is difficult to escape. The theory of 'Qwerty'[...] can also be extended into a general theory of social exclusion with far-reaching implications. The importance of institutions and of the specific history of a country in understanding events is given, for the first time, a powerful mathematical justification."*

Paul Ormerod in *The Guardian*

 ## Application

Increasing versus diminishing returns in management thinking

This section looks at the effects of the equilibrium mindset on decision-making in large organisations, contrasting it with the effects of positive feedback.

Negative feedback: the equilibrium mindset

Equilibrium is an unattainable ideal, and any attempt to reach it in the real world will inevitably be an inaccurate compromise. Nevertheless, the idea of equilibrium as the goal of human organisations made its way into so-called 'scientific management' (as part of the 'human as machine' approach of Taylorism) at the start of this century, and remains part of the 'dominant logic' of managers. As the table above points out, equilibrium has the status of a law in conventional economics and, in accounting practice, the need to 'balance the books' remains paramount. Equilibrium seems to fit the administrative mindset in public services: the "management of scarce resources", as Professor John Stewart calls it, appears to demand just such a balance. The problem with the 'equilibrium' mindset in the 'management of scarce resources' is that it makes the same assumption as classic economics: that there is a fixed quantity of something (in this case service provision, based on labour and materials, etc.) which can only diminish as it is used (either through wear and tear on equipment, consumption of materials, or the need for retraining, etc.). Application of these assumptions in the context of cuts can be disastrous, as the example below shows.

Cuts and the equilibrium mindset: diminishing returns
A public sector building repair depot was subject to cuts. A supermarket-style 'checkout' was introduced, to reduce 'shrinkage' and save money on staff, thereby theoretically increasing 'value for money'. At the same time, again to save on staff time, a 'no-returns' policy was introduced. This resulted in:

• massive queues at the checkout – up to one hour's wait for each worker in the queue
• massive increase in wastage – workers were given a bulk quantity to do even a small job and were not allowed to return the leftovers
• reduction in positive public perceptions of the depot – tenants would ring up saying 'Don't you want this back?' and be disappointed with what they saw as waste, even though the cost of collection would have been greater than the saving of 'wasted' materials.

The results were further diminishing returns, reduction in staff morale, resentment over the lack of trust shown by the new rules and further reduction in the already low public opinion of the service.

The paradox of feedback: the increasing returns mindset

Human systems can change their behaviour, unlike mechanical systems. A central heating boiler can't decide that it disagrees with the thermostat and make the room just a bit warmer, neither can an ecosystem decide to spare a few species from extinction. But human systems can change their behaviour; a manager can make choices about how to interpret feedback. Only certain sorts of complaints may be 'heard' and therefore acted on, while others are dismissed as frivolous or ignored because 'we'd like to help but it's outside our control'. Tom Peters urges us to welcome complaints and to encourage more of them in more and more detail.

"An organisation that perceives complaints as positive feedback is more likely to improve its service processes than one which views them as negative feedback. Creating a flood of information, whether deliberately or not, highlights the need for intelligence and learning to stimulate change and improvement."

Steve Trivett

An increasing returns mindset, on the other hand, sees all sorts of possibilities:

• new methods of work organisation
• user involvement in product and service improvement
• new partners
• networking
• empowered teams, etc.

When public service users are involved, a whole range of new possibilities start to emerge. Similarly, networking with other departments, bringing them into discussions about methods and procedures, can transform working relationships, even in a tightly specified contract. A grass cutting service was able to improve its service to schools by varying the nature of its work: leaving one area 'wild' on request to help generate a meadow ecology, mowing some areas more heavily for games but leaving a 'fence' of long grass to discourage dogs, swapping scheduled visits so that a mowing took place the day before an open day, etc. – all within its contracted yearly pattern of visits.

Lock-in at work: 'Why aren't you an Investor in People?'
The reader should be able to generate examples of lock-in from their own experience. One current example is described here.

Investors in People (IIP) is a UK quality assurance scheme for organisations which certifies that every employee is receiving training and development focused on the organisation's objectives. After a slow start, it now looks set to achieve lock-in. IIP was developed by the UK government of the day as part of its programme to improve Britain's global competitiveness. Many organisations have benefited from becoming 'Investors in People'. As more and more organisations gain the award, more and more organisations are encouraged to achieve it – that's increasing returns at work.

But there are also many organisations which already have their own excellent business-focused training and development schemes and will not benefit in any real way from IIP because, in effect, they are already

'Investors in People'. This is where we see the lock-in: some organisations are now finding that they are perceived to be inferior to competitors simply because they do not have the IIP award.

memes

It can also be illuminating to look at IIP as a meme, competing for space in the mind of organisations with other memes like Business Process Re-engineering.

 Cross-references

complex adaptive systems, system, perspectives, evolution of co-operation

 References

Brian Arthur, 'Positive Feedbacks in the Economy', *Scientific American*, February 1990, (also reprinted in *McKinsey Quarterly*, Number 1, 1994)

John Darwin, *The Wisdom Paradigm*, Sheffield Business School, unpublished paper, 1995

John H. Holland, *Hidden Order: How Adaptation Builds Complexity*, Helix Books, Addison-Wesley, 1995, ISBN 0201 407 930

Kevin Kelly, *Out of Control: the New Biology of Machines*, Fourth Estate, 1994, ISBN 1 85702 308 0

Paul Ormerod, 'Qwerty Input is Key Explanation', *The Guardian*, 22 January 1996

M. Mitchell Waldrop, *Complexity: the Emerging Science at the Edge of Order and Chaos*, Penguin, 1994, ISBN 0 140 179 682

Increasing returns and lock-in

The Web of Life

"The people who are living on this planet need to break with the narrow concept of human liberation, and begin to see liberation as something that needs to be extended to the whole of the natural world. What is needed is the liberation of all things that support life – the air, the waters, the trees – all the things which support the sacred web of life."
Haudenosaunee address to the Western World, 1977

"During rush-hour on the subway in Upper Manhattan straphangers were only mildly surprised to find a 90lb deer waiting outside their station. For the last five years wild turkeys, coyotes and deer have been moving south into populated areas of Westchester County and last year coyotes were found in the Bronx."
The Observer, 2 June 1996

"None of the various government systems humans have so far devised has enabled us to deal with the complexity of nature. Most of the problems we face today, in every field, are of our own making because the interconnectedness of mankind, our planet, and its resources is not taken seriously or even believed fundamentally."
Allan Savory, author of Holistic Resource Management

The Web of Life

The 'web of life' represents the interconnectedness that is perhaps the most striking and perplexing feature of living systems; the most complex systems in the universe. The interplay of agents in competition with each other creates the environments in which improvements continually evolve, in which organisms and organisations seek to preserve themselves against a background of constant change.

Ecosystem

Everything is connected to everything else. Boundaries are fuzzy. In an ecosystem, all actions can potentially affect all other things.

Coevolution

The concept of coevolution draws our attention to the power of interrelationships between entities. Coevolution is therefore an appropriate metaphor to inform our thinking about partnerships in all their forms.

Evolution of co-operation

Human society can be usefully described as playing games within games. Organisations need to be clear what strategies are needed for the types of situation in which they operate. Axelrod's work shows how, in initially competitive or antagonistic environments, co-operation can emerge for the benefit of all the players.

Fitness landscape

There is no such thing as a level playing field: instead we have constantly deforming landscapes. Success may come from actually ignoring some customers' needs – some of the time – and introducing new inputs into the system. In this perspective, strategy emerges from scanning not planning.

Autopoiesis

Autopoiesis addresses the mystery of life: how entities create and recreate themselves and their world. The concept of autopoiesis helps us appreciate the miracles of life and individuality. At the same time, it reminds us of the difficulty of real communication and how resistant to change any living system can be.

Ecosystem

Where is the boundary between ecosystems?

 ## Relevance
Everything is connected to everything else. Boundaries are fuzzy. In an ecosystem, all actions can potentially affect all other things.

Translation
There is no boundary

"Ecologists are forever troubled with the lack of sharp boundaries setting off one ecosystem from another. An owl flies out of a wood across an open field and somehow the reality of the different systems – the wood and the field – seems in doubt."

Niles Eldredge

autopoiesis

Being part of a system makes it difficult to see that system as a concrete entity. We have a strong sense of our own identity, with our skin defining the boundary between 'me' and 'not me'. But on a microscopic level, the boundary becomes very messy: for example, our skins are constantly losing dead cells. From the point of view of the microscopic mites that live on our skin and in our bed linen, there is no boundary.

"An ecosystem lacks components that could serve as a membrane against invasion by external species. New arrivals just wriggle into an ecological niche. Not every invading species will succeed of course. The ecosystem has 'casual edges' like the omni-distributed cohesiveness of a cloud."

Tyler Volk

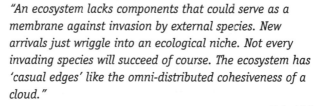
system

Throughout this book, the idea of the system is ever-present. In the entry on 'systems' it is stated that: "What is at stake is the defined boundary of the system". Unfortunately this idea breaks down completely when we look at ecosystems.

"I've just realised that an ecosystem is a system without an easily definable boundary."

Steve Trivett in a conversation with the author

evolution and coevolution

Ecosystems: 'Out of control'?

Kevin Kelly's book, *Out of Control*, gets its title from a play on words: biological systems are not 'under our control'. We are not 'in control' of them; they are 'uncontrollable' yet are by no means chaotic, dangerous or 'uncontrolled'. They are outside of our control, driven by a different kind of control that he calls 'co-control'. This is a perfect description of control in an ecosystem: how could it be otherwise in a system that does not even have a definable boundary?

Ecosystems: a global metaphor for a world without boundaries

The fragmentation of central and local government, the successive privatisations of the last decade, the new waves of quangos, regulatory and advisory, have massively increased the interconnectedness and complexity of the public sector in the UK. If the boundaries between the public and the private sector were ever clear, they are certainly not clear now.

And what of the voluntary sector and the privatised utilities? Parts of the voluntary sector look like parts of the private sector, while others compete (or co-operate) with local government in the delivery of services. In one region, 'youth work' has always been firmly within the voluntary sector, in another it is part of the work of a public sector department that also covers 'employment' and the 'environment'. It is simply not possible to draw a clear boundary around any of these sectors, any more than it is possible to dig up fertile earth without chopping one or two earthworms in half.

Here we suggest a single all-encompassing metaphor to guide organisations as we approach the millennium: ecosystem – to point up the fuzzy boundaries. The private sector, the voluntary sector and the local government sector are separate systems, just as a wood, an open field and a water meadow are separate ecosystems, but the boundaries between them are not clear. Any attempt to apply conventional systems thinking to them is therefore doomed to failure. Aspects of the ecosystem metaphor are described below.

Ecosystem: a global perspective
The Gaia Hypothesis of Jim Lovelock takes the idea of ecological interconnectedness to its ultimate conclusion: the earth's living and non-living components form an inseparable whole. Economies are going global. Very soon the planet will have a single economy, if that point has not already been reached. Only a global view of the work of an organisation will make sense in this context: our perspectives need to model the variety out there in the world, as Ashby's law of requisite variety reminds us.

system/system-in-focus

Ecosystem: everything is connected and changing all the time
Ecosystems are constantly evolving, new species moving in to new areas, old species dying out, new interdependencies forming and collapsing. The fitness landscape is continuously deforming. As in the boids simulation, the environment is mostly other actors. If you aren't involved in the game you won't understand it and you won't be successful in it. If an organisation delegates or contracts out its responsibilities for a service, it will very rapidly lose any understanding of what the customer needs from that service.

fitness landscape, self-organisation

Ecosystems are fragile: they can die
Ecosystems are fragile and can die but we don't fully know how or why. We know that ecosystems are

'sustained', but we do not yet know what 'sustainability' is. Ecologists speculate that the 'point of no return' has already been reached for several of the planet's rain forests. These forests may already be 'dead on their feet', past the point at which they can regenerate. What we do know about sustainability is that it is complex; regenerating an ecosystem is incredibly difficult because of interdependencies between species. 'Legacy species', keystone species and successor species all have to be introduced in precisely the right order. As Kevin Kelly says, it is not just a matter of a list of 'diversity', you also need the assembly instructions. In organisational terms Business Process Re-engineering (BPR) is a 'monoculture', and the majority of all BPR initiatives fail. The metaphor of BPR is the machine: it fails to acknowledge the complexity of the real world.

BPR failure: a study by Belmont and Murray in 1993, quoted by Eve Mitleton-Kelly, claims that over 50% of all BPR initiatives fail. Not only were the particular objectives of the re-engineering not achieved, but the disruption caused by the BPR undermined the well-being of the organisation. BPR doesn't just change structures, it changes networks of interrelationships, often to the 'point of no return'.

network and hierarchy

Valdis Krebs warns of the effects of the removal of links from a connected community. "Suddenly, its connectivity rapidly disintegrates leaving a dispersed 'archipelago' of relatively small sub-communities." Past a certain point, networks in organisations will simply fall apart. If we are to tinker with our existing systems, we need to be extremely cautious and humble.

In an ecosystem diversity is crucial
The perils of monoculture are well-known in agriculture. A single mutant strain of rice virus can wipe out half of the world's rice crop. (Almost the entire rice crop of Vietnam failed recently for just this reason.) It may be more 'efficient' to standardise on

one variety of cultivated grain but it is not wise. In nature there are always a million different tiny variations, any one of which may prove to possess the crucial resistance to a virus. Ecosystems are complex adaptive systems. So are organisations. It's time to realise the real truth of the statement that 'this organisation's greatest assets are its people'.

Application
Organisational ecology: failed transplantation
Ecologists know that all living creatures are interdependent. A native British oak supports over 400 different species; a Spanish oak imported into Britain supports less than 50. 'Not invented here' could be another way of saying that transplantation is unlikely to succeed.

coevolution

A home-grown change
A restaurant chain had appointed a new manager to one of its flagship properties. Unhappy with the existing shift system, and after wide consultation, she had improved performance significantly by bringing in a new system. Her senior management liked the new system so much that they adopted it throughout the region. (For more details see 'coevolution'.)

What happened at the other sites in the region?
The results were mixed: some improved and stayed at a higher level of performance; some improved slightly and then slipped back; others got slightly worse. There appeared to be a number of factors: the attitude of management, the degree of consultation, turnover in staff and so on.

Consider the organisation as an ecosystem
It is possible to explain all this from a standard management perspective, but consider this

complex adaptive systems

explanation. A restaurant is a complex adaptive system that is 'open' to its environment to a high degree (compared with, say, a finance company); its trade is based on customers who can observe most of its workings directly; its added value is quite intangible (ambience, atmosphere, even service quality are difficult to measure); its competitors are many and varied; its systems are complex and interwoven. In short, it is very similar to an ecosystem.

And if this comparison makes sense for a restaurant, it surely makes sense for large organisations, with their significantly greater complexity, interconnectedness, and high levels of accountability and scrutiny.

Permaculture management: applying sustainability ideas to organisations
Devon County Council, in common with many other local government bodies in the UK, has been busy in recent years applying the sustainability ideas advocated within Agenda 21. (Devon County Council is a regional tier of government in the south-west of England responsible for planning, education, and social services, etc. Agenda 21 is a United Nations initiative which promotes sustainable development.)

The two-day event 'Developing Sustainable Communities' is one example: in this case ideas from permaculture (an ecological approach to food production) are being applied to community development. Taking things a stage further, consultants working for the county are now developing new approaches to the management of organisations which are influenced by sustainability ideas.

Ecosystems mean business

In his book, *The Death of Competition,* James Moore argues that business should adopt an ecosystem model. His key case is Intel, which produces the chips inside most desktop PCs. He establishes how Intel 'grew' an 'ecosystem' in the computer marketplace, transforming itself from a relatively lowly position as one of several major supplier of chips to the once-mighty IBM into the centre of a coevolving network of businesses.

Moore describes a business ecosystem as a community of interacting organisations and individuals. This community produces valued goods and services for customers, who are also members of the ecosystem. Other 'member organisms' include suppliers, lead producers, competitors, stakeholders (including investors, owners, trades unions, trade associations) and other powerful 'species' such as government agencies, quangos and various regulatory bodies. The concept of the business ecosystem is therefore much broader than the idea of the 'extended enterprise' or the 'business sector'. Over time, the roles and relationships develop and coevolve between the 'species' and the 'direction' starts to be set by one or more 'keystone' species. The 'leadership' role may change over time but the role of ecosystem leader is valued by the community because it embodies a shared vision with which it can align, and offers a means to coevolve mutually supportive roles.

Strength in diversity

The strength of an ecosystem comes from the interconnections between its members, which develop entirely new possibilities for new organisms. In Central America the soil is very poor for ranching,

coevolution

yet the rainforest ecosystem that has adapted to that soil supports millions of diverse species. We can see a similar diversity in the massive growth in magazine publishing as a result of the invasion of PC-based DTP 'species' which are now similarly invading the World Wide Web ecosystem. As species diversity increases, the number of niches increases and the ecosystem as a whole flourishes.

From company to coevolution

Moore sums up his "new ecosystem-centred approach to leadership and strategy-making" as follows:

Issue	Company/industry view	Ecosystem view
Boundaries	Boundaries are 'givens'	Variable, to some extent a matter of choice
Primary unit	Industry or company	The business ecosystem
Economic performance is a function of	Internal management and average profitability of industry	How well alliances and relationships within the business ecosystem are managed
Central concern	Individual company growth	Development of, and position in, the economic network
Co-operation	Limited to direct suppliers and customers to maintain existing boundaries	Includes all players relevant to the search for ideas and unmet needs that can become part of the coevolving community
Competition	Seen as between products and between companies	Also seen as between ecosystems and for leadership within particular ecosystems

The four challenges of ecosystem coevolution

In Hawaii the *'ohi'a-lehua* trees colonise the new *'A'a* lava, their roots creating fine tunnels which connect the air pockets in the lava to create spaces for insects to inhabit. Soon herbivores and carnivores move in, creating richly canopied forest within a single human lifetime. The rules of ecosystem development are similar; they are what biologists call 'assembly rules'. Kevin Kelly describes how the key to re-establishing a prairie is the sequence of planting: just throwing down the 'right' mix of seed will allow the stronger plants to dominate, choking out the other species vital for the prairie ecosystem and producing only scrubland with low diversity. Once one species has occupied a niche, for example prairie songbirds, it is very difficult for another species to move in. Microsoft got an early start in the PC ecosystem when IBM licensed MS-DOS for their range of new personal computers. Microsoft's partnership with Intel (the 'Wintel' alliance) has allowed them to dominate the entire PC software industry; perhaps the only thing preventing them destroying all the competition is another powerful species: the US government with its anti-monopoly legislation.

Moore summarises the four stages of business ecosystem development as follows:

1. **Pioneering**: establishing a system and a sequence of symbiotic relationships that add new **value**.

2. **Expansion**: establishing **critical mass**; expansion across customers, markets, allies and suppliers.

3. **Authority**: leading **coevolution** and developing innovation in the system.

4. **Renewal: sustaining** continuous performance improvement.

Cross-references

metaphor, increasing returns and lock-in, network and hierarchy

References

Belmont and Murray, *Getting Ready for Strategic Change*, 1993, quoted in Eve Mitleton-Kelly, *Complexity and Learning*, unpublished paper, 1995

Niles Eldredge, *Reinventing Darwin*, Weidenfeld and Nicholson, 1995, ISBN 0 297 81603 9

Kevin Kelly, *Out of Control: the New Biology of Machines*, Fourth Estate, 1994, ISBN 1 85702 308 0

James Lovelock, *Gaia: a New Look at Life on Earth*, Oxford University Press, 1989, ISBN 0 19 286 030 5

James F. Moore, *The Death of Competition: Leadership and Strategy in the Age of Business Ecosystems*, John Wiley and Sons, 1996, ISBN 0 471 96810 2

Tyler Volk, *Metapatterns*, Columbia University Press, 1995, ISBN 0 231 06750 X

Coevolution

Relevance
The concept of coevolution draws our attention to the power of interrelationships between entities.
Coevolution is thus an appropriate metaphor to inform our thinking about partnerships in all their forms.

Translation

Evolution: don't all race, spread out!

Coevolution is a concept within the concept of evolution. Evolution (from the Latin *evolutio*, unrolling) is the theory which explains the mechanism by which species change and have changed since life first started on Earth. The overall trend in evolution is towards greater complexity and diversity of species. The familiar, and erroneous, view of evolution is of steady upward progress from fishes to amphibians to mammals to humans at the very peak of fitness. This view, with its in-built idea of hierarchy, is dangerously misleading; evolution is perhaps better viewed as a spreading-out like the creepers of a vine. Fitness in the biological sense is about adaptation to the environment, not how strong and fierce a creature is: in this sense of fitness as 'adaptation', insects and rats are much fitter than humans. 'Matchness' might be a better word to avoid the sense of superiority embodied in the term fitness. Fritjof Capra argues that:

network and hierarchy

> "*Detailed studies of ecosystems over the past decades has shown quite clearly that most relationships between living organisms are essentially co-operative ones, characterised by coexistence and interdependence, and symbiotic in various degrees. Even predator-prey relationships that are destructive for the immediate prey are generally beneficent for both species. This insight is in sharp contrast to the views of the Social Darwinists, who saw life exclusively in terms of competition, struggle and destruction. Their view of nature has helped create a philosophy that legitimised exploitation and the disastrous impact of our technology on the natural environment. But such a view has no scientific justification, because it fails to perceive the integrative and co-operative principles that are essential aspects of the ways in which living systems organise themselves at all levels.*"

Neo-Darwinian theory goes further, according to Capra:

"The classical theory sees evolution as moving toward an equilibrium state, with organisms adapting themselves ever-more perfectly to their environment. According to the systems view, evolution operates far from equilibrium and unfolds through an interplay of adaptation and creation. Moreover, the systems theory takes into account that the environment is, itself, a living system capable of adaptation and evolution. Thus the focus shifts from the evolution of an organism to the co-evolution of organism plus environment."

The Capra quotations above are taken from John Darwin's unpublished paper, *The Wisdom Paradigm*, used with thanks

Coevolution: the larger view

So the idea of evolution has itself evolved to produce the concept of 'coevolution'. Stewart Brand, founder of the *CoEvolution Quarterly*, offers these definitions:

"Evolution is adapting to meet one's needs. Coevolution, the larger view, is adapting to meet each other's needs."

attractor

The evolution of evolution sees the shift from the predator-prey relationship as 'survival of the fittest' implying that only rabbits lose if foxes eat all the rabbits, to a realisation that foxes will starve without rabbits. The history of evolution repeats a pattern again and again: organisms start out competing, then parasitism emerges and gradually turns into symbiosis. In many 'co-dependent' relationships in the natural world, the two parties can no longer survive without each other. The 'swollen thorn acacia' of eastern Mexico has lost its protective thorns and offers shelter and food to the acacia ant; in return, the ants repel all invaders, including the seedlings of other plants that would compete with the acacia. There are close

*evolution of
co-operation*

parallels in the world of organisations; we can observe partnerships and strategic alliances emerging from initial antagonisms.

John Holland describes coevolution in the context of complex adaptive systems like this:

> *"Organisms in an ecosystem coevolve. In the natural world, this has produced flowers that evolved to be fertilised by bees, and bees that evolved to live off the nectar of flowers. It has produced cheetahs that evolved to chase down gazelles, and gazelles that evolved to escape from cheetahs. In the human world, the dance of coevolution has produced equally exquisite webs of economic and political dependencies – alliances, rivalries, customer-supplier relationships, and so on. Coevolution is a powerful force for emergence and self-organisation in any complex adaptive system."*
>
> John Holland quoted in Waldrop

*evolution of
co-operation,
self-
organisation,
fitness
landscape*

Management aping nature

Complexity science is now beginning to unravel the underlying mechanisms of evolution and coevolution. Robert Axelrod's work on the evolution of co-operation has set out the mechanisms by which competitiveness gives way to co-operation. Simulations such as Tom Ray's 'Tierra', which reproduces the evolution of parasitism and symbiosis in 'code creatures' living in computer memory, and the 'boids' simulation of Craig Reynolds, convincingly demonstrate an understanding of some of the key processes of nature. In turn, their ideas are being applied to the management of organisations. Stuart Kauffman has developed extensive applications of the 'fitness landscape' concept – the 'space' in which the dance of coevolution is performed – to the area of technological competition.

Coevolution

Coevolution is everywhere

If there is one key idea in complexity sciences, it is 'co' as in coevolution. Complex adaptive systems are webs of interrelationships between yet more complex adaptive systems. Self-organised systems are co-dependent 'flocks' of agents. Examples will be found throughout this book.

Application

Coevolution and co-control

Kevin Kelly says that learning is overrated as the mechanism by which humans adapt and change. He describes coevolution as a powerful variety of what we know as learning, quoting Stewart Brand:

> *"Ecology is a whole system, all right, but coevolution is a whole system in time. The health of it is forward – systemic self-education which feeds on constant imperfection. Ecology maintains. Coevolution learns."*
>
> Stewart Brand

In the zone of complexity: co-control

The following exchange took place in an interview of Brian Eno by Kevin Kelly.

> *Eno: People tend to think that it's total control or no control. But the interesting place is in the middle of that.*

> *Kelly: Right. We have no word for that state of 'in-between control'. We have some words like 'management', or 'herding', or 'husbandry'. All these are words for co-control.*

> *Eno: I call it 'surfing'. When you surf, there is a powerful complicated system, but you're riding on it, you're going somewhere on it, and you can make some choices about it.*
>
> from an interview of Brian Eno by Kevin Kelly, published in *HotWired* on the Internet

Kelly prefers the terms 'co-learning' and 'co-teaching' to describe what the participants in coevolution are doing: teaching each other and learning from each other at the same time. This mutual 'education' of the coevolutionary players can clearly be seen in the game theory simulations of Robert Axelrod.

evolution of
co-operation

Coevolution in service delivery

In human systems, coevolution is about mutual adaptation and learning, even though each player will have different goals. The emergence of coevolution can be seen clearly in the case of a struggling school transport service. The service takes children with special needs to and from school, using a variety of transport, including taxis. The taxi drivers, wanting to minimise the number of trips they had to make whilst trying to maximise their fares, would make extra fares on the way to collecting the children. This made them late, causing great anxiety to school staff, parents and the children. At the same time, the service manager was trying to minimise the fares and maximise the promptness of the taxi drivers. (See note on 'optimisation' in 'fitness landscape' for an explanation of why neither can succeed in their aims.) The service manager brought in an organisational learning consultant who brought all the 'players' together (parents, schools, taxi drivers, service administrators, etc.) in 'team dialogue sessions' designed to engage the 'whole system' in solving the problems.

dialogue,
system

fitness
landscape

Punctuated equilibrium: shifting the patterns

Ilfryn Price and Ray Shaw of the Harrow Partnership have applied the concept of 'punctuated equilibrium', taken from theories of evolution, to issues of change management in organisations. Punctuated evolution is a theory which states that evolution goes in fits and starts rather than a smooth, upward progression of improvements. As complexity theorists remind us, most processes are messy, disordered and strange, and evolution is no exception. Millions of years can go by during which there is hardly any change at all: the same plants and animals just doing the same things over and over again, only to be disrupted by a 'brief' period of 'explosion' in which millions of new life forms suddenly appear as if from nowhere; hence the term 'punctuated equilibrium'. (By 'brief' we mean a few thousand years; in other words 'brief' in geological terms, not human terms.)

memes

Price and Shaw's approach involves the use of 'memetic change' concepts in organisations in a way that is analogous to genetic change in evolution. They call this sudden change "shifting the pattern".

Price says that:

> "For me 'Learning is Evolution' (a deliberate inversion of Bateson's 'Evolution is Learning'). In this view of the world, learning – like evolution – happens when equilibria are punctuated. I believe it is possible to do that in a way that encourages a beneficial learning (for people, the world, and a corporation or organisation). I also believe that the learning, like evolution, can be accelerated when the environmental shift that will enable it is created."

By the way, lest the reader be misled into thinking that Price is some sort of new Social Darwinist, be assured that he is just as opposed to such ideas as Fritjof Capra (quoted earlier).

He continues:

> "I am deeply sympathetic to the view, expressed most eloquently by Stephen Gould, that the comparisons may have done more harm than good. But at the end of the day, I draw a different message. I choose to believe that if

we can get a better understanding of the workings of learning as evolution we have a fighting chance of avoiding its worst outcomes."

Shifting the shift patterns: an example of punctuated equilibrium

A restaurant chain appointed a new manager to one of their flagship pub/restaurants: an ex-trainer, she was appalled by the effects of the entrenched shift system on the performance and well-being of the staff. The shift system had been in place for many years and nobody liked it. The shifts were long, tiring and unsociable, yet no-one wanted to change the system. After working there for several months and experiencing the effects of the system 'first-hand', on herself and her staff, she decided to act.

She made certain that she consulted everyone as she designed the alternative: they all were sure that they would suffer personally, although they could see that the change might benefit other staff. Convinced that she was right, and after being told that it was 'her risk' by her own manager, she went ahead and introduced her new system. The response was instant: everyone liked it and performance and morale immediately improved – much to the surprise of the 'gloom merchants' who predicted that the entrenched culture of the organisation would cause it to fail. Her senior management liked it so much, they ordered that the new system be adopted throughout the region, prior to being implemented nationally.

Note that this is not a Business Process Re-engineering (BPR) story. The system was not designed by external consultants; it was designed by an 'insider' who would suffer the consequences along with everyone else

Coevolution

inside the system. It was not based on computer modelling of workflow; it was not a 'big-bang' implementation. After it was introduced, it was changed several times, in minor ways, and continues to be amended in minor ways to take account of the differing needs of individual staff and the demands of service delivery. It is a system that is evolving organically.

Is it really all about culture?

Conventional management theory would find it hard to explain this overnight change. Theories of organisational culture suggest that entrenched attitudes are very resistant. These theories tell us that when change happens at all, it has to be pushed through using various 'change management' processes. Complexity theory, however, is very much in harmony with what happened in the restaurant case. We can see a 'punctuated equilibrium', in which one 'lock-in' is exchanged for another. The pattern of staff attitudes is very reminiscent of a strange attractor in a 'dynamical system' when the system 'jumps' suddenly from one 'track' to another. This rich set of complexity metaphors offers a range of insights into change in human systems. To find out what happened next see 'ecosystem'.

increasing returns and lock-in

attractor

ecosystem

Cross-references

evolution of co-operation, self-organisation, fitness landscape, attractor

R | References

Fritjof Capra, *The Turning Point: Science, Society and the Rising Culture*, Flamingo, 1983, ISBN 0 00 654017 1

John Darwin, *The Wisdom Paradigm*, Sheffield
Business School, unpublished paper, 1995

Brian Eno interviewed by Kevin Kelly: archives at the
HotWired web site: http://www.hotwired.com

Kevin Kelly, *Out of Control: the New Biology of
Machines*, Fourth Estate, 1994, ISBN 1 85702 308 0

James F. Moore, *The Death of Competition:
Leadership and Strategy in the Age of Business
Ecosystems*, John Wiley and Sons, 1996, ISBN 0 47
196810 2

M. Mitchell Waldrop, *Complexity: the Emerging
Science at the Edge of Order and Chaos*, Penguin,
1994, ISBN 0 140 179 682

The evolution of co-operation

 Relevance

Human society can be usefully described as playing games within games. Organisations need to be clear what strategies are needed for the types of situations in which they operate. Axelrod's work shows how, in initially competitive or antagonistic environments, co-operation can emerge for the benefit of all the players.

Translation

Why isn't it a completely 'dog eat dog' world?

If we believe the cynics, everyone is out for themselves. This can't be completely true: there are islands of co-operation and partnership everywhere we look. Companies are increasingly making 'strategic alliances', especially in the high-technology field, for example the Wintel grouping (Microsoft Windows software and Intel computer chips).

coevolution, ecosystem

In the beginning, however, there tends to be competition and conflict based on suspicion and ignorance. Michael Lissack quotes March and Simon, saying that the central task of an organisational manager is "the delicate conversion of conflict into co-operation". The gradual emergence of effective partnerships in the UK between local government and the TECs ('Training and Enterprise Councils' created by the previous UK government's privatisation programme), is an excellent example of the 'evolution of co-operation' from an initial position of mutual distrust.

So where does it come from, when there is no central authority and nobody is in charge of the game? How does it get started – and most important of all – how, in the 'Age of Partnership', can we do it better?

Game theory, which is the mathematical study of games and strategy, has had little to say about these complex issues until the recent work of Robert Axelrod.

Nice guys finish first

In his book *The Evolution of Co-operation*, Robert Axelrod explains in detail the development of co-

The evolution of co-operation

operation in superpower politics, private enterprise and local and national government. To paraphrase Richard Dawkins (in the introduction to Axelrod's book), this is an idea of optimism; a believable, realistic optimism, more satisfying than religious optimism because it acknowledges the fundamental realities of human nature. Life, as we know it, means 'Darwinian' life: which unfortunately means 'that which survives', whatever it takes. From this deeply pessimistic beginning, which assumes great selfishness and indifference, Axelrod is able to demonstrate the emergence of 'something that is in effect, if not necessarily in intention, very close to amicable brotherhood and sisterhood'.

The 'prisoner's dilemma'
A simple gambling game, the 'prisoner's dilemma', has played a key role in Axelrod's work. It is the key to understanding his ideas. As the name suggests, it was based on the idea of two prisoners arrested and thrown into separate cells who had to choose whether to 'grass' on their friend or not. The problem for each of them being that the other one is making the same decision: to 'grass' or not. If both hold out, they get reduced sentences; if one 'grasses up' the other he goes free, but if both 'grass', both get long sentences. In the jargon, it is a **zero sum game** (a win-lose game is an example). Strategic analysts, economists and games theorists love this game for the same reason that most people will dismiss it: it's a pure abstraction and real life isn't like that. What Axelrod saw, however, was that when the game is 'iterated' (the scientist's word for a game played with many turns or 'goes') for a **large** and **indefinite** number of turns, it demonstrates convincingly that co-operation is the

the 'game of life'

winning strategy. (An iterated game with an indefinite number of turns is a **non-zero sum game**. As James Carse points out in his book, *Finite and Infinite Games*, 'life is a non-zero sum game', and the majority of our interactions in real life are of the non-zero sum type, also known as 'win-win' games.) Only in a one-off game does it make sense to 'beat' the other player. The basic gambling version of the prisoner's dilemma works like this:

There is a banker, and two players: A and B. Each player has only two cards: a 'co-operate' card and a 'defect' card. To play, both players place their chosen card **face down** at the same time. Then the banker turns them over to reveal who has won or lost. There are four cards (2 x 2) and therefore four possible outcomes, as follows:

Outcome 1: Both play 'co-operate'. Banker pays both players $300, the 'reward for mutual co-operation'.

Outcome 2: Both play 'defect'. Banker fines both players $10, the 'punishment for mutual defection'.

Outcome 3: A plays 'co-operate', B plays 'defect'. Banker fines A $100, the 'punishment for being a sucker', and pays B $500, the 'temptation to defect'.

Outcome 4: The reverse of Outcome 3. A defects and wins $500, B is the sucker fined $100.

It doesn't actually matter whether the amounts are fines and rewards, nor does the exact amount matter. What does matter is that there is a ranking order to the possible payoffs:

The evolution of co-operation

Very good	'temptation to defect'	500
Fairly good	'reward for mutual co-operation'	300
Bad	'punishment for mutual defection'	-10
Very bad	'punishment for being a sucker'	-100

(There is also another, more technical condition: the average of the 'temptation' and 'sucker payoff' must not be better than the reward for defecting, otherwise the incentive to risk defection is diluted.)

Now let's show why, like in the earlier case of the prisoners in their cells, the best strategy is always to defect, using the payoff matrix below:

	B co-operates	**B defects**
A co-operates	good **REWARD (R)** for mutual co-operation **$300**	very bad **PUNISHMENT (S)** for being a sucker **$100 fine**
A defects	very good **TEMPTATION (T)** to defect **$500**	bad **PUNISHMENT (P)** for mutual defection **$10 fine**

Defect: you will, you will, you will...
To understand the dilemma, you need to put yourself in the situation and think 'What if?' Imagine you are player 'A'; if you think B will **defect**, then your choices

are in the second column: to either defect or not, being fined $10, or worse, $100. But what if B **co-operates**, shown in the first column. Well, if you co-operate (which is nice) you get $300, but if you defect you get even more – $500! So the best thing to do, regardless of what B does, is to defect, and oddly enough B will reach just the same conclusion about you. So you will defect every time; yet you both know that if you both had co-operated you could have taken $300 each off the bank. That's why it's a dilemma!

It works just the same for the prisoners: defect by 'grassing' your friend and if he is dumb enough to co-operate and not 'grass you up', he goes down for a long time and you get out. Co-operate, and they can't prove either of you guilty of the big crime, so you both get a short sentence. If you both defect and 'grass' on each other, you both get a stiff sentence, but not as bad as when one of you grasses the other. The pay-off matrix is identical, even though the 'currency' is jail sentences – the rank order is the same. There is no way out of it; your best move is to defect and 'grass' each other, because there is no way of ensuring agreement, no way of ensuring trust.

Go on, nobody will ever know...

There can't be any trust if the game is only played once; this is what the 'one-off' prisoner's dilemma demonstrates. Think about being on holiday in another country. You are in a shop in a town you know you'll never visit again, and you are given the wrong change: the change from a 20,000 note rather than the 2,000 you tendered. The temptation, however fleetingly, will flicker across your mind. But back home, in your local shop, you won't think twice about pointing out the mistake, because... Good question. Why? There are

The evolution of co-operation

lots of possible reasons: you don't want to be thought a cheat; you like the shopkeeper; you don't like the shopkeeper and you want to feel superior; because honesty is the best policy; because there is trust between you. Whatever the reasons, the scenario is an iterated game; you'll be in the shop again for another turn tomorrow, so what you do today will affect what you do tomorrow. Or to put it another way, thinking about tomorrow (the next time in the future) affects your decision today. In a wonderfully evocative phrase, Axelrod calls this the **'shadow of the future'**, and it is one of the keys to the evolution of co-operation.

Let's look at the possibilities in the iterated prisoner's dilemma. After ten turns (iterations), A could be holding $5,000, but only if B was silly enough to play 'co-operate' every time A played 'defect'. If A and B really started to trust each other they could clean up by taking $300 apiece off the banker each go. But that isn't very likely at first, because the temptation to defect ($500, remember) is great; so every so often A will defect, as will B and both will be fined, sometimes $10, sometimes $100 if they both defect together. So what's the best strategy? Is there a reward on earth for being nice? This was precisely the question that Axelrod set out to explore: he set up a computer-based tournament for strategies, inviting mathematicians, psychologists, computer experts and political scientists to submit strategies in the form of programs. These were 'run' on his computer against each other, and against copies of themselves over and over, until all 15 strategies had played each other 200 times.

Don't do it to them before they do it to you

The various programs were allowed to 'remember' what happened in previous goes; they were also allowed to use 'the flip of a coin' (random choice) as part of their strategy. Axelrod included his own program 'random' as a baseline to judge the others against: it simply played at random each time, so a strategy which couldn't beat 'random' was a pretty poor one. The winner was 'tit for tat', the simplest strategy of them all. Tit for tat consists of two rules:

• co-operate the first time you meet
• after that, do whatever they did to you on the last go.

Richard Dawkins, in his book *The Selfish Gene*, explains why tit for tat is always the winner, using a strategy he invents called 'naive prober'.

When tit for tat plays with naive prober, the game will look just the same as tit for tat playing with itself, except that once in a while naive prober defects and collects the $500. Naive prober has done well, but tit for tat obviously retaliates on the next go, so naive prober similarly retaliates on the next go, and so on, the result being that both do less well than they would by co-operating. (Each gets an average of $250 per move, rather than $300 for co-operating.)

The key to tit for tat's success lies not in beating the others, but in **persuading the others to behave in a way that allows both to do well**. Michael McMaster, in a posting to the Learning Organisation email discussion group, points out that:

> *"The game does not present co-operation as the 'obvious' choice. The most common choices are figuring out ways to take the high prize by exercising non-co-operation."*

The evolution of co-operation

As Axelrod explains:

> "In a non-zero sum world you do not have to do better than the other player to do well for yourself. This is especially true when you are interacting with many different players. The others' success is virtually a pre-requisite for doing well yourself."

'Nice'

The many complex strategies used in the computer tournament have some characteristics in common: one of these is a category that Axelrod calls 'nice'. Tit for tat is an example; it is 'nice' because it only defects in retaliation. He also describes a category he calls 'forgiving (strategies in games)' – a strategy which 'forgets' defections done to it after a while. That niceness wins came as a surprise to many of the experts who were used to devising ever-more cunning and subtly nasty strategies. In a repeat of the tournament, despite the best efforts of the 'nasty' programmers, the nice guy, tit for tat, still finished first, and not only that, tit for tat turns out to be 'robust': a strategy which does well in many situations. It also has many lessons for organisations, some of which are explored below.

Complex adaptive systems: competition and co-operation

Patterns of behaviour in complex adaptive systems arise from competition and co-operation among the agents themselves. Competition can produce a very strong incentive for co-operation, as agents spontaneously forge alliances and symbiotic relationships with each other for mutual support. Competition and co-operation are closely interrelated: alliances emerge at every level and in every kind of complex adaptive system, from biology to economics to politics.

complex adaptive systems

Society in silico

Axelrod and others have developed computer models in which 'generous tit for tat' (a variant of the original that forgets past wrongs after a while) becomes the dominant strategy in a simulated ecosystem, subject to a certain level of mutation being present. Susan Forrest, of the Santa Fé Institute, has modelled a complete 'society' in a computer simulation as part of the SFI's research into complex adaptive systems. Using vast numbers of concurrent players ('citizens'), each player plays the prisoner's dilemma with the other 'citizens' that are in close proximity, over and over again. The results of the simulation are encouraging: most players eventually 'discover' or 'learn' and adopt a co-operation strategy in relation to the 'society' as a whole.

This account of Axelrod's ideas is necessarily very brief and only the most basic ideas have been covered; the work is continuing, broadening its application into more complex situations of partnership and competition, in collaboration with the Santa Fé Institute.

 ## Application

Playing games: new forms of co-operation

When we think of co-operation, we tend to think of co-operation between partners – people with the same interests. For example, a quality group within a sales department. But co-operation is now much more complex: it is not simply co-operating with colleagues; it now involves co-operating with competitors – 'co-opetition' to use that inelegant neologism.

This new form of co-operation is no longer about simple common interest based on a common

perspectives

ecosystems

perspective; it is now focused on compromise and mutual benefit for different players – a 'symbiosis' to use a biological metaphor. (James Moore's book *The Death of Competition* explores the idea of 'business ecosystems'.)

Sometimes competition will appear relevant, at other times co-operation seems right. The ideas of James Carse on the nature of games will be useful when thinking about strategies within partnerships with both the community and competitors. Carse's book *Finite and Infinite Games*, suggests that competition is healthy and successful in what he calls 'finite games'. On the other hand, co-operation is healthy and successful in 'infinite games'; and he reminds us that all finite games are played within infinite games.

Two kinds of games
Carse points out that:

> There are at least two kinds of games: finite and infinite.
>
> A finite game is a game that has fixed rules and boundaries and is played for the purpose of winning and thereby ending the game. It is a win-lose, zero sum game; an example is contract bidding.
>
> An infinite game has no fixed rules or boundaries. In an infinite game you play with the boundaries and the purpose is to continue the game. It is a win-win, non-zero sum game; for example, working with the community.
>
> Finite players try to control the game, predict everything that will happen, and set the outcome in advance. They are serious and determined about getting that outcome. They try to fix the future based on the past.
>
> Infinite players enjoy being surprised. Continuously running into something one didn't know will ensure that the game will go on. The meaning of the past changes, depending on what happens in the future. (continued)

Finite players are serious; infinite games are playful.

All games are inherently voluntary. There might be consequences of not playing, but there is always a choice required. Driving on the right side of the road, shaking people's hands, and paying taxes are games one has a choice about playing. There are certain rules and boundaries that appear to be externally defined, and you choose to follow them or not. If you stop following them you aren't playing the game any longer.

There is no rule that says you have to follow the rules.

All finite games have rules. If you follow the rules you are playing the game. If you don't follow the rules you aren't playing. If you move the pieces in different ways in chess, you are no longer playing chess.

Infinite players play with rules and boundaries. They include them as part of their playing. They aren't taking them seriously, and they can never be trapped by them, because they use rules and boundaries to play with.

In a theatrical play, the actor knows that she really isn't Ophelia. The audience knows that she really isn't Ophelia. But if she does a good job, Ophelia can express herself through the actor. The playing is most enjoyable when it is both clear that it is chosen play, that the actor is doing it voluntarily, and at the same time it is convincing, following the rules so well that it seems real.

You can play finite games within an infinite game. You cannot play infinite games within a finite game.

You can do what you do seriously, because you must do it, because you must survive to the end, and you are afraid of dying and other consequences. Or, you can do everything you do playfully, always knowing you have a choice, having no need to survive the way you are, allowing every element of the play to transform you, taking pleasure in every surprise you meet. Those are the differences between finite and infinite players.

Summary by Flemming Funch from his website:
'WorldTransformation/ NewCivilisation/WholeSystems'
http://www.worldtrans.org

The evolution of co-operation

Tit for tat in service delivery

coevolution

A clear case of tit for tat can be seen in the case of the struggling school transport service referred to earlier ('co-evolution in service delivery' in 'co-evolution', p.188). Because of poor service, complaints were rising, and unfortunately the situation was such that negative relationships started to develop. The team was trapped in an escalating tit for tat, in which angry complaints led to excuses not to respond (not responding = 'defect'), which in turn led to escalation of the complaints, and so on. The process only stopped when the complainant gave up. This is a classic 'game' of tit for tat, and the solution, once the hard work of engaging with the problem has been done, is simple: stop 'tatting' and let the other 'players' know that you have stopped (principally through your behaviour towards them). This is exactly what the team dialogue process enabled the team to do.

Co-operation can emerge if the rules change

Trading Standards work is a public sector function carried out in the UK by local government. Until recently its work has not involved much contact with the 'general public'.

A Trading Standards section in a local government agency had developed detailed procedures around the ISO 9000 quality standard to support criminal and civil investigations. This largely involved quantitative research techniques. When faced with the need to listen to users of the Consumer Advice Centre, after a departmental reorganisation, the staff found themselves having to unlearn their assumptions. New thinking was required to organise for face-to-face dialogue with people likely to be very critical of the service they were providing. The rules had changed: a group of solo professionals now had to work as a team.

> *"Suddenly team interactions became the key to success. I wasn't prepared and had to readjust how I worked. This was difficult: at times I felt exposed, all at sea, but the support I received was great and we are now beginning to collaborate after years of competing with each other."*
>
>
> Trading Standards Officer

network and hierarchy

How to encourage co-operation in networks

Networking and partnership are increasingly part of the global business environment. Here Ilfryn Price, Senior Lecturer in Facilities Management at Sheffield Hallam University, gives some advice, excerpted from the forthcoming book *Shifting the Patterns*, on creating and encouraging co-operation in networks, based on Axelrod's four principles:

1. **A likelihood of repeated interactions.** If any player knows the game is ending, or if it is reduced to a one-off contest, the rewards for defection are always likely to be too great.

2. **A positive sum for the game as a whole.** If the net reward for collaboration is no more than the gain to one player from defection, no collaborative strategy can win.

3. **A sufficient future value in collaboration.** Collaborative strategies do well because they set out to lock future rounds of the game into a win-win rather than a win-lose or lose-lose equilibrium. If future reward is discounted too highly, if in effect too high an interest rate is applied to calculate the present

The evolution of co-operation

discounted value of a future return, then sacrificing current earnings doesn't pay.

4. **Swift, but not continued retaliation.** The tit for tat strategy minimises its exposure to defectors by retaliating immediately, but does not then bear a grudge provided the other player does not continue playing defect.

He then adds a fifth condition for organisations:

self-organisation

5. **The need for a 'critical mass'.** In a complex system, an adequate number of operators (or agents) are needed without which useful work cannot commence; activity is then merely random.

Discouraging co-operation
A 'co-operative network' that someone doesn't like gets called a cartel. Axelrod's work is equally applicable to situations which require the blocking of co-operation that would lead to disbenefit for end users, as in the context of service contracts. In order to discourage co-operation, just reverse the advice.

Cross-references
complex adaptive systems, ecosystem

References

Robert Axelrod, *The Evolution of Co-operation*, Penguin, 1990, ISBN 0 14 012495 0

James Carse, *Finite and Infinite Games*, Penguin, 1987, ISBN 0 14 009399 0

John L. Casti, *Paradigms Lost*, Carnival, 1989, ISBN 0 7474 0967 6

Richard Dawkins, *The Selfish Gene*, Oxford University Press, 1989, ISBN 0 19 286092 5 (chapter 12, 'Nice guys finish first')

Michael R. Lissack, *Chaos and Complexity: What does that have to do with Management?*, unpublished 1996 paper available at website: lissack.com/writings

Tom Lloyd, *The Nice Company*, Bloomsbury, 1990, ISBN 0 7475 0346 X

James F. Moore, *The Death of Competition: Leadership and Strategy in the Age of Business Ecosystems*, John Wiley and Sons, 1996, ISBN 0 471 96810 2

Ilfryn Price and Ray Shaw, *Shifting the Patterns: Transforming the Codes of Personal and Company Performance*. (For further details contact the Harrow Partnership, Pewley Fort, Pewley Hill, Guildford, Surrey GU1 3SP, UK)

The evolution of co-operation

Fitness landscape

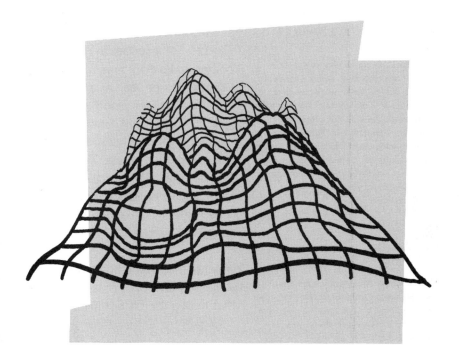

Relevance

There is no such thing as a level playing field: instead we have constantly deforming landscapes. Success may come from actually ignoring some customers' needs – some of the time – and introducing new inputs into the system. In this perspective, strategy emerges from scanning not planning.

Translation
Fit for climbing rubber mountains

A fitness landscape is a mountainous terrain showing the locations of the global maximum (highest peak) of fitness and the global minimum (lowest valley). Fitness is a biological concept which describes the relative 'success' of a species in relation to others in its environment. So fitness can be seen as a measure of how well an 'actor' is adapted to its niche in the landscape.

The height of a feature is a measure of its fitness. The term, first used by Wright in the 1930s in the field of evolutionary biology, has been greatly expanded by complexity researchers.

Like fitness landscapes, possibility space is another concept derived, by way of complexity science, from the mathematical concept of a 'search space': a space in which the solutions to equations may be located in a three-dimensional graphical form. Possibility space is an extended metaphor for both the exploration of possibilities and the design of space for the creation of possibilities. One could say that fitness landscapes exist in a hilly part of possibility space.

possibility space

The material in this section is taken from Michael Lissack's unpublished 1996 paper *Chaos and Complexity: What does that have to do with Management?* Please note: the material has been edited and given new headings in some cases.

Competition between businesses can be said to occur on a fitness terrain: that terrain itself is not fixed but changes by 'deformation' in response to the effects of the actions of all the other actors, as if it is made of rubber. As in the boids simulation, the environment is mostly other actors. It can be compared to walking about on a children's bouncy castle: each time you find a place to stand, someone else will join you, which means you both start to sink into a hole: you can't stay on top by standing still, you have to be searching constantly for a new place to stand. (We can also view industrial competition as the interactions of independent agents in a complex adaptive system. A fitness landscape is another way of looking at the same system.)

self-organisation

complex adaptive systems

Fitness landscape

> *"Fitness landscapes in evolution and economies are not fixed, but continually deforming. Such deformations occur because the outside world alters, because existing players and technologies change and impact one another, and because new players, species, technologies, or organisational innovations enter the playing field."*
>
> Kauffman and Macready

coevolution

Fitness landscapes change because the environment changes. And the fitness landscape of one species changes because the other species that form its niche themselves adapt to their own fitness landscapes.

> *"We can construct such a landscape for any system of connected interactions (such as a firm and its environment), and it is the presence of 'conflicting constraints' that makes the landscape rugged and multi-peaked. Because so many constraints are in conflict, there are a large number of rather modest compromise solutions rather than an obvious superb solution."*
>
> Stuart Kauffman

The attraction of the peaks

attractor

We can literally turn the idea of the 'fitness peak' on its head to give us the idea of a 'basin of attraction'. The term 'basin of attraction' is often used to depict the idea that systems drift down into the attractor state from their initial position. In the 'ice-cream attractor' described in the 'attractor' entry, once the two ice-cream sellers are at the midpoint, they are stuck at the bottom of the 'basin of attraction', which is another way of saying that they are stuck on a hilltop in the fitness landscape: they cannot leave their local hilltop to migrate to another higher hill, much as they might want to (except of course when the landscape deforms, as mentioned above). The 'basin of attraction' idea in relation to attractors reminds us that the end state of a system is largely involuntary; the ice-cream sellers just 'end up' where they are, because that's how it happens, they don't necessarily make conscious choices.

A 'fitness peak' is an upside-down 'basin of attraction'

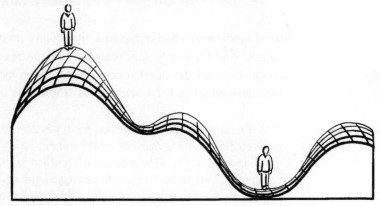

Keeping fit in a deforming landscape: what's the strategy?

One of the key roles of a manager is to lay out strategy for his or her organisation. But what is a strategy?

> *"What is a strategy? Once upon a time, everybody knew the answer to this question. A strategy specified a pre-commitment to a particular course of action. Moreover, choosing a strategy meant optimising among a set of specified alternatives, on the basis of an evaluation of the value and the probability of their possible consequences. Optimising pre-commitment makes sense when a firm knows enough about its world to specify alternative courses of actions and to foresee the consequences that will likely follow from each of them.*

When the foresight horizon is clear, it may be possible to anticipate all the consequences of any possible course of action, including the responses of all other relevant agents, and to chart out a best course that takes account of all possible contingencies. As foresight horizons become more complicated, the strategist can no longer foresee enough to map out courses of action that guarantee desired outcomes. Strategy then must include provisions for actively monitoring the world to discover unexpected consequences, as well as mechanisms for adjusting projected action plans in response to what turns up.

In contexts like this, the relation between strategy and control is very different from the classical conception. It is just not meaningful to interpret strategy as a plan to assert control."

Lane and Maxfield

Strategy: observation, not control

Thus, in a complex world, strategy is a set of processes for monitoring the behaviours both of the world and of the agents of the organisation, observing where attractors are and attempting to supply resources and incentives for future moves. Command and control is impossible (at least in the absolute and in the aggregate), but the manager does retain the ability to influence the shape of the fitness landscape.

"Adaptive organisations need to develop flexible internal structures that optimise learning. That flexibility can be achieved, in part, by structures, internal boundaries, and incentives that allow some of the constraints to be ignored some of the time. Properly done, such flexibility may help achieve higher peaks on fixed landscapes, and optimise tracking on a deforming landscape."

Stuart Kauffman

Kauffman's use of the term 'optimisation'

Kauffman is talking locally not globally. Optimisation as a goal for the whole system is a failed linear concept; local optimisation is a concept drawn from complex adaptive system theory, which contends that global optimisation is impossible. Kauffman's point is that each 'unit' must try to optimise. Optimisation is only achievable temporarily at a local level, not permanently across a whole entity. Kevin Kelly, in the seventh of his Nine Laws of God in his book *Out of Control*, explains that:

complex adaptive systems, network and hierarchy

"For instance, an adaptive system must trade off between exploiting a known path of success (optimising a current strategy), or diverting resources to exploring new paths (thereby wasting energy trying less efficient methods)."

Application
'Good enough'

The ideas of Herbert Simon will be familiar to many people in public administration. Simon invented the term 'satisficing' to describe the juggling act that all public administrators have to perform: the balance between giving people what they want and enough to satisfy their requirements. In some ways, Kauffman's ideas represent a full-circle return (with added depths of complexity) to Herbert Simon's ideas of 50 years ago: both Kauffman and Simon would agree that attempting to optimise a system is counter-productive.

We could also add that complexity science tells us that balance is a fiction; there is only dynamic stability at the 'edge of chaos'.

The more general term 'good enough' comes from D.W. Winnicott, the British psychoanalyst who advocated 'good enough' parenting; he knew that a failing parent is a poor parent: better to be 'good enough' than fail to achieve perfection.

the 'edge of chaos'

So what suits everybody is a compromise for the common good: it may not be what perfectly suits you.

Fitness landscape

*perspectives/
management
and the
'modern
paradigm'/
rationality*

Sir John Harvey-Jones tells us that "the best is the enemy of the good". This is the dilemma of satisficing. Later Simon realised that the capacity of the public administrator to make 'rational' decisions based on 'all the facts' was more limited than he first thought. He called this idea 'bounded rationality'.

Kevin Kelly asked Simon what he felt about the drive for greater efficiency and the elimination of errors from production. Simon replied that it could be done, but he questioned whether it could be done profitably. He said: "If you're interested in profits, you have to 'satisfice' your zero-defects." In other words, you can't achieve your goals if you aim for perfection. Kelly describes this as the 'complexity tradeoff'.

'Good enough' is the natural strategy in living systems

*complex
adaptive
systems*

Complexity theory strongly supports Simon. It tells us that human systems, like living systems, can be considered as complex adaptive systems, in which survival is more likely if there are multiple goals rather than one 'best' goal. Because the environment is constantly changing, it is not possible to select one approach and stick to it. The system must 'loosen up' to allow a range of competing strategies to emerge. At any moment in time, some strategies will be performing better than others: these can be encouraged, but the others should not be eliminated completely; elements of them may be needed sometime later. The analogy is to a gene pool, which needs a level of variation to stay healthy and avoid inbreeding. In human systems, 'groupthink' can be considered to be the inbreeding of ideas.

coevolution

Not simply the best: applying 'good enough'

The concept has obvious application in a number of settings were the temptation is to go for 'the best': quality management, decision-making and any situation where resource allocation is an issue. Don't ask, 'What's the best way?' ask, 'What might be good enough?'

An example: dealing with complexity and avoiding the 'one best' solution

Public transport agencies in the UK frequently have to deal with very emotive requests for pelican crossings because people may have been injured or killed crossing the road. Requests for crossings are dealt with using the official Department of Transport formula. A calculation is made based on the number of pedestrians crossing the particular road against the number of vehicles using it. The 'rules' don't have to be interpreted rigidly: many agencies also take into account accident figures, even if the criteria imposed by the formula are not fully met. The quandary for the engineer is to locate the crossing in a position where it will be most used, given the local circumstances, road conditions, previous accident sites, etc. Rather than trying to reduce the problem down to its constituent elements, traffic engineers decided to consult with a wide range of local residents and road users: in other words they chose to make their task even more difficult. By engaging with complexity, they were able to take account of local politics and objections as part of the decision-making process, not as an add-on. Thus they were able to find a 'good enough' solution that would work because it had local support, rather than an 'optimum solution' suggested by statistical research and formulae without reference to people's wishes and feelings.

complexity

Fitness landscape

But these ideas do not apply to you, do they?

Michael Lissack's paper, *Chaos and Complexity*, focuses on two cases: one an Internet content provider (a start-up with fewer than forty employees) and the other a large division of a biotechnology company. But it would be a mistake to think that the fitness landscape idea does not apply to your organisation, just because you aren't a 'high-tech start-up' in Silicon Valley. The global environment for organisations is increasingly competitive, and sectors which were traditionally 'safe' are now under attack. The best example is probably the break-up of the telecoms monopolies: starting in the US and the UK in the 1980's. What we are now seeing is a global 'media inversion' in which telephony goes broadcast and broadcasting becomes personal with web pages 'pushed' to your PC desktop via satellite.

How to develop adaptive organisations the Kauffman way

How can we create flexible internal structures that optimise learning? The key variables which complexity research seems to suggest are important in answering this question are:

1. Defining the size and number of business units.

2. Defining the nature of interactions among these units.

3. Arriving at a shared language or other mechanism for information to be passed among and processed by these units.

4. Defining a strategy for 'search' – the hunt for improvements out amongst the fitness landscape, and

5. Making room for and use of 'noise'.

Kauffman carried out a number of studies of search on rugged landscapes which demonstrated that, when fitness is average, search is best carried out far away across the space of possibilities. But, as fitness increases, the fittest variants are found ever closer to the current location in the space of possibilities.

On complex surfaces (i.e. rugged fitness landscapes with many hills and valleys) systems can become trapped on poor local optima (the wrong hill). Kauffman's research has developed a variety of approaches to 'simulated annealing' to assist in getting organisations away from these local optima and moving toward a more global optimum.

"Simulated annealing is an optimisation procedure based on using an analogue of temperature, which is gradually lowered so that the system nearly equilibrates at each temperature and is gradually trapped into deep energy wells. The general concept lying behind simulated annealing is that at a finite temperature the system sometimes 'ignores' some of the constraints and takes a step the 'wrong way', hence increases energy temporarily. Ignoring constraints in a judicious way can help avoid being trapped on poor local optima."

Stuart Kauffman

"Kauffman suggests how to organise communication based on the difficulty of the problem being confronted. In simplistic terms, simple problems can be dealt with by formal systems where large wholes are controlled, and difficult problems can best be dealt with by many small teams with minimal communication between each."

Michael McMaster in a posting to the Learning Organisation email discussion group

A patchy approach

One procedure, derived from simulated annealing optimisation ideas, Kauffman calls 'patches' – partitioning a system on a complex, rugged fitness landscape into independent departments, or patches, each of which thereafter optimises selfishly. Because the departments are independent and selfish, actions by one department to improve itself can move the entire system the 'wrong way' (that is, not in the

Fitness landscape

corporately approved direction) hence those independent actions can allow the entirety to avoid bad local minima.

Kauffman suggests that decentralised, flatter organisations might actually be more flexible and carry an overall competitive advantage. (By 'decentralised', Kauffman means an organisation broken into 'patches' where each party attempts to optimise for its own selfish benefit, even if that is harmful to the whole. By 'flatness', Kauffman means an organisation designed around a relatively flat fitness landscape – one without many jagged peaks and valleys, but not a flat plain either.) Such a structure can lead, he says, as if by an invisible hand, to the welfare of the whole organisation.

autopoiesis

The successful reorganisation of Southwark's Housing department (a UK public sector housing agency) is also a good example of patch-based improvement, as well as an example of change in a resistant, 'autopoietic' system.

Patches aren't business units

network and hierarchy

Kauffman emphasises that these patches must interact. Thus, this advice is clearly different from the old management standby of the independent self-sufficient business unit. He finds that the organisation as a whole can be moved toward a global optimum even though each patch is acting selfishly, but only if the nature and quantity of the interactions between them are appropriate. Interactions require a mechanism of fairly continual communication. He stresses that the patches must be 'coupled'. In management language, the units

dialogue, possibility space

must communicate, and not just at quarterly review sessions.

The concept of receiver-based communication is inspired by Kauffman's ideas, and is in itself a continual communication system, but between individuals rather than units.

receiver-based
communication
(RBC)

coevolution

"The basic idea of patch procedure is simple: take a hard, conflict-laden task in which many parts interact, and divide it into a quilt of non-overlapping patches. Try to optimise within each patch. As this occurs, the couplings between parts in two patches across patch boundaries will mean that finding a 'good' solution in one patch will change the problem to be solved by the parts in adjacent patches. Since changes in each patch will alter the problems confronted by neighbouring patches, and the adaptive moves by those patches in turn will alter the problem faced by yet other patches, the system is just like our model coevolving ecosystems."

Stuart Kauffman

Kauffman further finds that as coupling increases and thus drives the system towards chaos, an ameliorating effect is derived by slicing the system up into smaller patches. In other words, "hard problems with many linked variables and loads of conflicting constraints can be solved by breaking the entire problem into non-overlapping domains. Further […] as the conflicting constraints become worse, patches become ever more helpful".

Manage data by ignoring some of it
Kauffman's other two procedural suggestions are: first to ignore some of the inputs coming into the organisation (the theory seems to be that accommodating all inputs leads to freezing and that the degrees of freedom necessary to better find optima can only be accomplished by deliberately ignoring some of the inputs). Secondly, it is necessary to recognise that too much data ceases to be 'information' (that which informs the agent or actor) but instead acts like a brake on the system. This second idea he calls 'tau' – his measure of how many simultaneous changes an

Fitness landscape

interacting system can tolerate before freezing up. This clearly translates into a warning about customer service: let it become an obsession, to the extent that it is the only focus of the organisation, so that the staff are neglected or punished in the pursuit of it, and the overall level of customer service will fall. Kauffman's figure is still a high one, however (around 90%), so this is not a 'do your own thing and ignore the public' type of message.

> *"While simulated annealing is an important mathematical optimisation procedure, it involves agents making errors 'on purpose' at a controlled diminishing frequency. People and organisations do not appear to behave this way. On the other hand, human agents in organisations almost certainly respond to the stresses of conflicting demands by ignoring some of the constraints some of the time. Such apparent irresponsibility can [...] work to the overall benefit of the organisation."*
>
> Stuart Kauffman

Ignoring some of the information being generated allows for a new set of priorities to emerge and, at least some of the time, a significant improvement can result.

Guastello refers to this as the 'chaotic controller'.

Chaotic controllers are based on Ashby's law of requisite variety, which is an engineering principle that posits that the controller of a system needs to be at least as complex as the system it intends to control. "Chaotic systems obviously need something special. Chaotic control works counter-intuitively by first adding a small amount of low-dimensional noise into the system. The reasoning is that the amount of sensitivity to initial conditions is not uniform throughout the attractor's space; sensitivity is less in the basin of the attractor and least in its center . . . Adding noise to the system allows the attractor to expand to its fullest range."

Fitness landscape

It's not noisy enough around here

Kauffman describes the role of error and of ignoring some constraints. The annealing process can also be looked at as one of deliberately introducing 'noise' into a system to see what happens. By noise we mean different ideas, which may or may not be connected to the focus of the unit in any obvious way, and different perspectives.

perspectives

This is a very different concept to the traditional view of noise as a random problem to be minimised. Where traditional managers may have wished to delete the extraneous, the manager educated in complexity research may wish to cause the deliberate addition of 'noise' at various places along the way.

The appliance of complexity science: other metaphors

A useful summary of other complexity concepts and their metaphorical application to the work of organisations will be found in the 'metaphor' entry in this book.

metaphor

 ## Cross-references

perspectives, coevolution, possibility space, metaphor, network and hierarchy, dialogue, attractor

 ## References

Stuart Kauffman, *At Home in the Universe*, Oxford University Press, 1995, ISBN 0 19 509599 5

Kevin Kelly, *Out of Control: the New Biology of Machines*, Fourth Estate, 1994, ISBN 1 85702 308 0

Michael R. Lissack, *Chaos and Complexity: What does that have to do with Management?*, unpublished 1996

Fitness landscape

paper available at web site: lissack.com/writings

References cited by Lissack in the above paper:

Guastello, S., *Chaos, Catastrophe and Human Affairs*, Lawrence Erlbaum Associates, 1995

Kauffman, S., and Macready, W., 'Technological Evolution and Adaptive Organizations', in *Complexity*, Vol.1, No.2, 26-43, 1995

Lane, D., and Maxfield, R.,1995, 'Foresight Complexity and Strategy', *Santa Fé Institute Working Papers*, #95-12-106

Michael McMaster, *The Intelligence Advantage: Organising for Complexity*, Butterworth-Heinemann, 1996, ISBN 0 7506 9792 X

Autopoiesis

The hedgehog: attempting self preservation whilst scanning its environment

 ## Relevance

Autopoiesis addresses the mystery of life: how entities create and recreate themselves and their world.

The concept of autopoiesis helps us appreciate the miracles of life and individuality. At the same time, it reminds us of the difficulty of real communication and how resistant to change any living system can be.

Translation

When a judge criticises some aspect of the legal system, other judges listen. When Richard Rogers knocks modern architecture, architects can't avoid paying attention to his ideas. But when Trevor Nunn, respected theatre impresario and artistic director of the UK's Royal National Theatre, sounds off about litter and homeless people begging and sleeping in doorways, he is savaged in the press, except for some other theatre people who offer him support. And when a government attempts to reform the police force, the response from the police is, 'What do they know about our work?'

What's going on here is autopoiesis in human systems. In the above examples, we can see both communication and the lack of it. To understand what is going on, we first need to look at autopoiesis in living things: a complex and mysterious idea, which nevertheless offers many rich insights, only a few of which are explored here.

> *"The greatest problem with communication is the illusion it has been accomplished."*
>
> George Bernard Shaw

Autopoiesis in living systems: the miracle of me

Autopoiesis means 'self-making' – it is the process by which living creatures constantly recreate and maintain themselves and their own identity. Maturana and Varela, the two Chilean biologists who invented the concept, describe living creatures as "characterised by their continual self-production". You may be familiar with the idea that the atoms in our bodies change completely over a number of years but if this is true, why am I still me and you still you? Shouldn't we feel increasingly 'different' as time goes by? Because as physical entities we are completely different, not one atom of our bodies is the same as before, yet we have an unbroken sense of self going back to our earliest memories. Autopoiesis is the process by which this miracle is achieved.

Me and not me: the boundary of the self
Think about a cell; it could be a cell in your liver, or a single-celled animal like an amoeba, or a plant cell. Every cell has a cell wall, a membrane, a boundary that separates it from everything else outside of it. In the case of a cell in your liver, 'outside' merely means other nearby liver cells; in the case of the amoeba everything outside of it is the entire rest of the world. This boundary is part of the cell, it is not something separate. It simultaneously limits and therefore defines the cell and it takes part in all the processes of the cell. If it was just an inert boundary, the contents of the cell would flow out like water from a leaky bucket when the membrane was damaged. So the membrane is crucially part of the cell, and when the membrane is damaged the cell's processes will quickly act to keep out everything that is not the cell ('not me') and keep in everything that is part of the cell ('me'). This is the real mystery: how does a cell achieve this 'closure', when part of itself forms the boundary between itself and everything else? How does it know the difference between 'me' and 'not me'? Please don't expect an answer here: the key point is that this 'self-production' – this 'closure' between what is 'me' and what is 'not me' – is a key characteristic of all living systems. Autopoiesis is a genuinely new way of looking at systems: the insights to be gained by viewing human interactions from this new standpoint are potentially enormous.

Autopoiesis applies to all living systems

system

Autopoiesis is also a characteristic of organisms: there are many millions of cells in an organism, all organised into sub-systems within the 'big system' that is the individual. Autopoiesis also applies to systems of organisms: herds and flocks, populations and entire species. And, because organisations can be viewed as collections of organisms (human beings, for example), autopoiesis is also being applied to social systems like governments, companies and professions.

The autopoietic system

The complex adaptive system

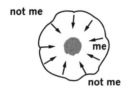
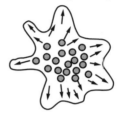

The diagram on the left represents autopoiesis as an 'inward urge': a self-preserving tendency to retreat to the core of the identity. The shape is intended to be reminiscent of an amoeba retracting itself inwards; the arrows indicating this 'pulling in'. It is a characteristic of a system as an individual entity, preserving itself.

This is contrasted with the 'outward urge' of the complex adaptive system shown on the right. The 'outward urge' is a characteristic of the individual elements, 'agents' or sub-systems, within a system. The difference is about focus. When the focus is on the system as a single entity we need to be aware of autopoiesis. When we focus on the individual elements in a system we need to be aware of the system as a complex adaptive system, containing many independent agents, each seeking to improve their situation. This is represented by the 'pushing out' of the arrows.

complex adaptive systems

The internal model determines the response

Because any autopoietic system has a sense of 'me and not me', we can also say that any autopoietic system has an internal model of itself and its world. Take the example of a muscle cell in the leg of a marathon runner: at the start of a race, complex carbohydrate molecules in the cell's environment will be ignored in preference to simple sugars. But at the end of the race those same carbohydrates will be seen as 'emergency food' because the cell will be running low on energy.

So when a cell responds to a molecule, it is the cell's internal model that determines its response, not the nature of the incoming chemical. It is not a simple case of 'stimulus and response', it is instead the interactions within an incredibly complex internal organisation responding to its own internal needs. When we think about internal models we are usually talking about people or organisations, yet even the simplest cells like bacteria have some knowledge of their world. As Stuart Kauffman points out, *E. Coli* has a model of its environment that allows it to understand that if it swims upstream in a glucose gradient it will find more food.

Do try this at home: demonstrating autopoiesis in your visual system

It's a bit like a teacher at school wandering around with a 'kick me' notice pinned to his back by some naughty schoolboy: he wonders what the sniggering is about because he doesn't know what he doesn't know.

Maturana and Varela emphasise that our view of our world is controlled by our internal model of the world, and not by incoming data. They have an elegant interpretation of the familiar blind spot experiment which they use to point out that "we can't see what we don't see". To experience the effect for yourself, look at the diagram opposite.

Autopoiesis

Instructions: Turn the book around and hold the page about one foot (30 cm) away from you, with the cross on the left and the circle on the right. Cover your left eye and stare at the cross.

Turn

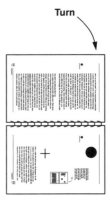

After a while the black spot will disappear! (It will reappear if you glance to the side, so keep your eye focused on the cross.) The usual explanation is that the black spot is falling on the area of your retina where the optic nerve emerges, which is not sensitive to light. OK, but what Maturana and Varela ask is this: 'If that's true, how come we don't go around with a hole that size in our visual field all the time? Our visual experience is of a seamless, non-holey space: why don't we see the hole?' If our visual system worked like a camera (that is if it were a simple mechanical image processing system) and we painted a spot on the lens we'd see it in the viewfinder, and it would appear on every picture. But our eyes aren't like a camera; our visual system is in fact an extension of the brain: it has tremendous 'brainpower' of its own, which it uses to 'fill in' the hole for us using its internal model of the world so that we 'do not see that we do not see'. So we inhabit our model of the world, in which there are no blank areas floating in front of our eyes, not the world 'out there'. As they put it "...we do not see the 'space' of the world, we live in our field of vision..." Every time you talk to colleagues about 'what just happened at that meeting,' where everyone seems to have a different idea of 'what was going on', you should acknowledge that we all live in different worlds.

perspectives

You don't see what you don't see

Let's explore this visual model a little more. Think about what is happening at the back of your eye when you move your head slightly: the image on the retina changes. Move your head an inch while you are looking at the diagram, and the cross moves an inch on the retina. If you stand up and spin round slowly the image will also 'pan' across your retina. So why don't you see the movement? We already know the answer: your visual system 'stabilises' your view using its internal model of the world around you. This trick has now been copied by the latest camcorders: they have anti-roll mechanisms that use a slightly earlier image to cover up the blurred part of a recording caused by camera shake: in other words they no longer record exactly what they see. Without your eyes performing a similar trick all the time, your world would be as blurry and confusing as a drunken amateur video of a back yard barbecue.

Autopoiesis

What IBM and E.Coli have in common

In a very real sense, all living systems, from IBM to *E.Coli*, 'imagine' themselves and their world. This concept challenges the very core of our sense of reality: we experience the world as something solid 'out there', yet Maturana and Varela tell us that we never really experience a world 'out there'. What we experience is our model of the world 'in here', based on its interpretation of data from 'out there'. They also point out that "we cannot know what we don't know", in just the same way as we cannot see what we don't see in terms of the 'hole' in our visual system.

Murray Gell-Mann, Nobel Prize-winning physicist and founder of the Santa Fé Institute, likes to be described as the 'discoverer' of the quark, an elementary sub-atomic particle. His colleagues at SFI like to tease him by saying that he didn't discover the 'quark' he invented it. Gell-Mann insists that 'the truth is out there'.

"There's a circular or network process that engenders a paradox: a self-organising network of biochemical reactions produces molecules which do something specific and unique: they create a boundary, a membrane, which constrains the network that has produced the constituents of the membrane. This is a logical bootstrap, a loop...[it] is precisely what is unique about cells... [Bootstrapping is] a nice way of talking about this funny screwy logic where the snake bites its own tail and you can't discern a beginning. Forget the idea of a black box with inputs and outputs."

Varela

Implications of autopoiesis

In our work in organisations, we act as if we believe that people behave 'rationally'; we see communication as a straightforward matter of talking or sending out memos, and training as mainly about input. Autopoiesis challenges these ideas about human interactions in profound ways. Let's summarise the key points:

perspectives/ rationality

• an organism has an internal model of its world
• a boundary is created and maintained that is part of the organism itself.

The following conclusions flow from this view:

- We don't experience the world directly by receiving incoming data. Our internal model is an incredibly complex internal 'structure' responding to its own internal needs. This internal model of the world determines our response, not the input. Organisms are not reducible to black boxes with inputs and outputs: they are **self-referential** systems.

- We preserve ourselves: we are 'conservative', we resist change, and when forced to change, we respond in such a way as to maintain our unbroken sense of self. (This can be more easily seen in other people: for example, when we point out that someone has changed their mind on a subject, they will usually disagree.) Changes are incorporated and then forgotten about (when asked where we got an idea from, we usually don't know and have to guess, or try to reconstruct how it came to us – 'It must have been on that seminar last year...'). This 'conservation of self' is a good thing, of course. Without it we would be prey to whatever strange ideas are floating around at the time. Do we really want people in organisations to be always chasing the latest fad?

memes

- We are really only interested in what we are interested in, or what we need to be interested in, and not much else. So we will only learn what we want to learn, and we will fit it into our existing view of the world. If the training requires us to change or abandon our world view, we will tend to reject it.

perspectives

These points lead us to a healthily pessimistic view of human communication as innately difficult, and human behaviour as both self-determined and resistant to external changes.

Autopoiesis

The autopoietic nature of communication

When I turn to someone over samosas and warm chicken legs at a seminar lunch, and I don't know who they are, my view of them will change in some way if I discover that the person is a chief executive, and equally, if I discover that she is knowledgeable about complexity theory, or uses a Macintosh computer.

When you read that first sentence in the paragraph above (the one that mentions samosas and chicken legs) you may have noticed the word 'she', and a few words after, the words 'chief executive', and then the word 'computer'. You may have been slightly surprised; after all there are few women chief executives, and few Macintosh users. You could in fact be wondering what the sentence is doing there at all. It doesn't seem to belong. You may also have wondered if you had read the sentence somewhere else recently. If you read the 'Landscapes of Possibility' section before this one you will have read it there in the entry on 'perspectives'. Or you might just be wondering what this 'samosas and chicken legs' stuff is all about. Those feelings of surprise, bewilderment or irritation are 'perturbations in your system'. A perturbation is a disturbance; in this case the perturbation was something unexpected in your reading. It was unexpected because it did not fit your internal model, which would not include samosas and warm chicken legs as likely words to occur in this discussion of communication.

Perturbations in the night

If you wake up in the middle of the night hearing a strange noise, you will be perturbed. Your mind starts to scan, sending out patterns looking for a match. 'What was that noise?' 'Must've been next door's cat; hold on, that doesn't sound like a cat; maybe it's a burglar'. When we finally decide that it was a cat, or a fox or something, the scanning stops and we drift back to sleep.

Your noise is perturbing my system

The concept of autopoiesis can transform our understanding of communication between human beings. If we accept autopoiesis, we must also accept the power of the boundary between the system of the self and the outside world, and we must therefore view communication not as something 'natural' and commonplace, but as a process inherently difficult, fraught with obstacles and complications. We must see our utterances for the noises that they are. If our utterances make sense to others they will be acknowledged as speech rather than just noise or babble. Speech is noise that means something to someone. If our utterances catch the attention of another 'system', if they 'resonate' with that system, rather than just perturbing it, communication may start to happen. In the lunch example above, I pay attention to chief executives in particular, because they represent a potential opportunity to promote my organisation at the top level of one of our customer organisations. I pay attention to people who are interested in Macintoshes and complexity theory because I am interested in Macintoshes and complexity theory. Both are instances of my internal model at work – interested in what it is interested in – self-referentiality.

Information that makes a difference

What is information in an autopoietic system? It is not simply data: we have already established that data will be ignored if the internal model isn't interested in the input. At best a data input will cause a perturbation in the system. To get inside the system, data has to make a difference to the system, literally. Information is "a

Autopoiesis

difference that makes a difference", as Gregory Bateson puts it. Let's take the example of complexity theory from the lunchtime chat above, and let's imagine that I already know that Stuart Kauffman's book *At Home in the Universe* is out in paperback. As we chat, you tell me that Kauffman's new book is now out and on sale in bookshops. I assume that you mean his third book, which had just been published in hardback in the US. This data certainly makes a difference to me: I'm ready to rush down there and buy it, until you tell me that it's called *At Home in the Universe* and I realise you're talking about his second book. This is not information. I already knew that. It does not make a difference to me. A lot of so-called information in organisations is like that: as the boss unveils some new plan, we ask ourselves what difference will this make, and ignore it.

A new model of communication
To reach a new understanding of communication, we need first to examine the deficiencies of the traditional models of communication. A basic communication model looks something like this:

Basic communication model

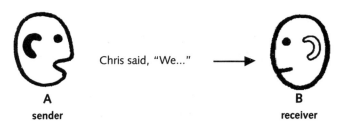

Chris said, "We..."

A
sender

B
receiver

What we see here is an ordered world: I am talking, you are listening. When I stop, you will start, and so our conversation will go on, in this orderly predictable manner. It is a black box model as in the illustration above, derived from information theory: input to B; output from A. A is active, B is passive, as indicated by A's open mouth and 'closed' ear, and B's 'open' ear and closed mouth. When used on training courses on communication or groupwork, the model is often modified by the inclusion of the 'message received' message, to acknowledge that the 'receiver' has an active part in communication, rather than just being a passive receiver.

Modified communication model

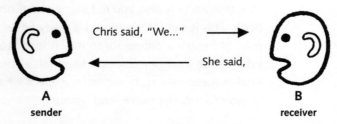

A
sender

B
receiver

In the modified communication model, we see both parties are active, as indicated by the open mouths and 'open' ears. This model might appear to work quite well, especially when it is being applied to formal settings like presentations, management briefings or training courses. These are highly structured, controlled settings, which tightly specify the type of contribution people can make and the timing of it. 'I'll take questions at the end... I'll just finish the last slide and then we can...' It rarely works out like that though does it? Either no-one responds, because they've all fallen asleep, or they start arguing about some obscure point that has nothing to do with what your important presentation was about...

Orderly communication
We can describe this model as being about highly **ordered** communication. The fate of our highly ordered communication in the example above is

Autopoiesis

chaotic irrelevance or **static** ignorance. In complexity theory, **order** is class 2 behaviour, **chaos** is class 3, and **stasis** is class 1. Tightly controlled situations will not stay tightly controlled: they either break down into chaos or freeze up in stasis. As is argued elsewhere, class 4 – **complexity** – is the desirable state because it allows information to be exchanged and learning and adaptation to take place.

the 'edge of chaos'

We can also view this model as hierarchical and paternalistic: it is a top-down model ('Look at me when I'm talking to you') which assumes that the speaker knows best ('I'm telling you what you need to know'). Talking has higher status than listening, which is relegated to acknowledging receipt of my important words.

dialogue

This paternalistic top-down model of communication fails to convey the messiness and difficulty of human communication. In this inadequate model, the speaker behaves like a parent talking to a child: paradoxically, all the emphasis is on the sending of messages by talking, even though the model is totally dependent on the other person listening.

Look at me
Children are often maligned as bad listeners (we'd expect them to be, given the nature of autopoiesis) but child psychologists, playworkers and anyone who has spent time around other people's children will have noticed that children do in fact listen very carefully to what is said to them, just not in the way we would like. When a parent talks to a child they will be hoping that their words will 'sink in' and be acted upon: 'Look at me, if you don't tidy your room, you can't go to the cinema tonight.'

Are you listening to me?

What the child is often doing is better described as 'monitoring' or 'scanning': they compare what they hear with their internal model of the parent and if it's just the usual stuff, they'll mumble OK and ignore it completely. When being told off for destroying the stereo, they will listen very very attentively, not to the words, but to the possibility of something unpleasant happening to them. When they hear, 'but this time I'll forgive you', they immediately switch off. It's true, nobody really listens to a word you say. That's autopoiesis for you: self-referentiality, self-preservation, self-interest. (It isn't just children who have cause to monitor the speech of others: it is anyone in a subordinate position in an organisation or in society at large.)

This 'scanning' of the 'utterances' of the other person for relevance is the core of an autopoietic model of communication.

An autopoietic model of communication

dialogue

In the autopoietic model, the players actively 'scan' around them. In the illustration below, we see four people at a party or similar social gathering. A is gossiping to C about Brian, her boss at work; B is chatting to D about his new car while scanning the surrounding conversations.

Scanners on

The scanning is shown as 'radar beams' being sent out, not from the person, but from their internal model of themselves. This scanning is autopoiesis at work: my system is constantly scanning for anything that might interest me – or affect me in some way – threats, opportunities, food, stimulation. The best example of this scanning, which is based on patterns generated by the internal model, is the well-known 'cocktail party effect'.

An autopoietic model of communication

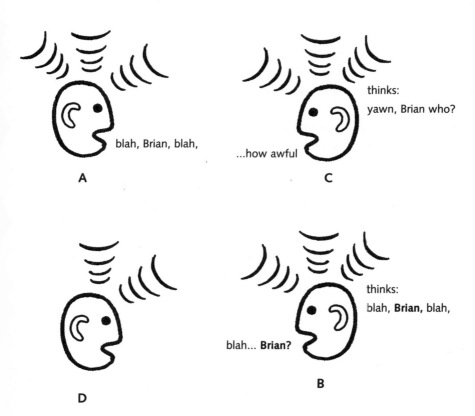

A

blah, Brian, blah,

...how awful

C

thinks:
yawn, Brian who?

D

blah... **Brian?**

B

thinks:
blah, **Brian,** blah,

Are you talking to me?
This is shown in the diagram above: A has mentioned 'Brian' her boss at work; B, whose name happens to be Brian, has picked his own name out of the babble around him, because along with myriads of other

patterns, he is constantly scanning for the pattern of his own name. This scanning is not passive: the radar is a 'smart radar'; it knows the pattern of the things it is looking for. The scanning is active because the patterns are being sent out into the world, looking for a pattern out there that matches them. (Michael McMaster describes this as the mind, or the nervous system, generating possibilities in the form of very fine 'oscillators' that are looking for a match. In linguistic terms, these might be words, phrases, sentences or images, although scanning is not confined to words and images; the oscillations are much more basic and lower-level than language.)

Desperately seeking Brian

The mind hunts for those incoming 'signals' for which a 'resonance' can be readily established. We can think of this resonance in musical terms: sending out the note C and getting a C reflecting back is not interesting. Getting random noise back is unusual but not interesting. Getting an E back is interesting because it resonates to form a chord. Where there is no resonance, the mind will ignore or avoid any more of that stream of incoming signal. Where there is resonance, it follows the path towards its source. In the example above, Brian has just heard his own name; he will listen for a while until he realises that he isn't being talked about, then he will resume his general scanning. We can say that his system was perturbed by the pattern of his own name, but no resonance took place.

Deep and disorderly conversation

Complexity is inherent in this autopoietic model of communication: in the party example, the topics of conversation will emerge in a random way, from perturbations in the systems of the participants. One person mentions another, someone else mentions an idea that I've just read about, and the discussion evolves from these beginnings. In a group discussion (a formal team meeting, or an informal lunchtime chat with colleagues) people will be talking over each other, not listening to the person currently 'holding forth', listening to someone else, making asides to the person next to them, and so on. This is the reality of language in a group, however much trainers and managers wish it were more orderly and controlled.

The next generation
Actually, the process is orderly and controlled, which should please trainers and managers. There is a self-organising process controlling the emergence of the conversations similar to the process by which a flock is formed from the application of simple rules within the environment of the flock. A conversation is generated as the outcome of a series of game-like iterations, each 'conversant' responding to the responses of the others.

self-organisation

evolution of co-operation

Processing the process
The issue is not, 'How can we impose order on this mess?', but rather 'Is this process giving us what we need? Is it getting there eventually?' We need a certain patience and humility, because as has already been said, attempts to control lead to stasis or chaos not the order we desire. Learning and adaptation happen under complexity: class 4, somewhere **between** order and chaos. The self-referential, autopoietic model of communication is much closer to the messy, incomplete, and complicated nature of communication than the crude black box idea of the computer-based information scientists.

Together we can resonate: the emergence of communication

Meanwhile back at the party, if it actually is Brian that A is talking about, Brian will continue to listen, and will 'follow the path towards its source'. He may move closer to A, who we will now acknowledge as 'Alice', in recognition of the importance of identity to every autopoietic system. This is shown in the diagram below.

Resonance in the autopoietic model

Brian said, "We..."

A
me, myself, Alice

blah, blah, that's...

blah, Brian blah,

B
me, myself, Brian

In the diagram, the scanning has changed. Brian is focusing on Alice, and she is reciprocating. Brian may now speak to Alice, following up what she is saying. If what he says is of interest to her, that is, if the pattern he sends resonates with the patterns she is scanning with, then she will enter into conversation with him. They will tune into each other in a complex iterative process. This is how communication emerges between autopoietic systems.

Autopoiesis

"Sending and receiving is a rather old-fashioned and mechanistic view of communication. It's a view that, in my experience, gets organisations into all kinds of trouble. A dialogue or a conversation occurs in (or emerges from) the interaction of two or more people, and the idea of sender and receiver is neither technically accurate nor, in my opinion, a very powerful interpretation. Nothing is communicated directly to another. All [utterances] go through the interpretation processes of context, meaning, significance, content, etc. Even apparently sensible speaking is frequently merely noise to its intended recipient. You may choose to call yourself the 'receiver' but what is occurring is not a linear process. For communication to take place on any scale worth talking about, it will be 'iterative generation' towards a shared understanding. The understanding of both the originator – 'sender'? – and others will alter as the process progresses. Until we begin to give up the mechanistic metaphor of sending and receiving as the basic mode of communication, we aren't going to crack the problems we keep confronting."

Michael McMaster in a posting to the Learning Organisation email discussion group

Application

Autopoiesis is particularly relevant to two key topics in organisations:

• change, and
• communication.

Autopoiesis and change in resistant systems

Professor Hari Tsoukas has analysed political change in a number of European countries, including Germany, Greece and the UK. The Greek government has several times attempted massive legislative changes similar to those made by the Thatcher administration in the UK, without success. How did Thatcherism succeed where others failed?

(The following material is based on his presentation 'Reforming Social Systems: Coping with Self-reference', given at the LSE 'Strategy and Complexity' lecture series in June 1996, but the interpretation offered here is that of the present author.)

According to Tsoukas, the key lies in the nature of social systems. They are autopoietic systems; which is to say they are highly self-referential. Like all autopoietic systems, they constantly recreate their boundaries and their identity and they act to resist change.

The characteristics of 'self-referential social systems'
The following can be applied to 'self-referential social systems':

• social systems possess certain shared understandings which are expressed as sets of language-based distinctions, for example, the world view of a professional, expressed in jargon

• the understandings possessed by individuals within social systems are based on 'social practices'

• 'social practices' are complex coherent forms of social activity, bound by rules.

Not all social activities are 'social practices' in this special sense. For example, football, architecture and farming are social practices, whereas a 'kickabout' game in the park, bricklaying and planting cabbages are not. There must be a set of coherent rules, developed and extended over time by the participants. (This idea is similar to the definition of a profession, except that it is wider.) The identity and distinctiveness of a practice is derived from within it and rooted in the experience of it. Architects define architecture, making clear distinctions between it and neighbouring activities such as 'construction'. Nursing is defined by nurses and when outsiders try to understand what motivates nurses they will fail. Without the relevant experience

Architecture, in turn, defines architects: the latter are socialised into the language of architecture through the practice of architecture.

of a social practice you will be incompetent to judge it. Within the practice are a number of 'internal goods': the reasons why the insiders engage in the practice. Nursing defines nursing: it is a 'self-referential social system' – a system which has created its own model of reality. The system is autopoietic: it interacts with its model, not directly with the real world.

The statements below, used elsewhere in this book, should now be explicable in this context:

When a judge criticises some aspect of the legal system, other judges listen. They are all insiders inside the 'self-referential social system' of the law.

When Richard Rogers knocks modern architecture, architects can't avoid paying attention to his ideas. Like the lawyers, they are constrained by the 'self-referential social system' in which they practise.

But when Trevor Nunn, respected theatre impresario and artistic director of the Royal National Theatre, sounds off about litter and homeless people begging and sleeping in doorways, he is savaged in the press, except for some other theatre people who offer him support. Nunn is speaking outside of his own social practice, he is intervening in someone else's social practice; what is more, it is a hotly disputed terrain, uneasily shared between the police and the social services, and other practitioners.

And when a government attempts to reform the police force, the response from the police is, 'What do they know about our work?' Police chiefs quickly point out the effects of 'external goods' brought to bear on their self-referential system.

'Internal goods'

In this imaginary dialogue the nature of some of the 'internal goods' of policing is revealed.

Government: The police need to be efficient in order to fight crime effectively.

Police: Our role is to soothe conflict and solve local problems. We can't avoid responding to whatever concerns people when they contact us. That's why we have 'beat bobbies'.

Government: That's not very efficient, let's introduce police cars, so that you can fight crime faster.

Police: Without knowledge of the local patch that we used to get from bobbies on the beat, we can't do very well.

Government: Use paid informers and computers; we'll measure your efficiency with clear-up rates and other statistics.

Police: How many arrests do I have to make to pay my mortgage? How do we measure the effect of a young officer soothing an old lady who has lost her cat? We have to have the trust of our communities in order to fight crime. Policing is by consent, our role is to soothe conflict and solve local problems.

Policing is defined by the police and when governments try to perturb the system, it will resist.

Thatcherism: a lesson in how to reform self-referential social systems

Tsoukas suggests that the two crucial factors in reforming self-referential social systems are: a) supplying information to a system in a way which forces it to respond, and b) providing a context for making sense of that information.

Autopoiesis

This new context is an alternative model of reality, based on a new set of linguistic distinctions. The information needs a context, an alternative model of reality, based on a new set of linguistic distinctions: new words, new reality. Margaret Thatcher had first to 'plausibly retell' the story of Britain since the second World War, in order to begin the process of change. Then new information was introduced in such a way that it could not be ignored by the targeted systems, such as school league tables, hospital waiting lists, crime clear-up rates, cost comparisons between local government services nationally. The recipients complained loudly, but they could not ignore the comparisons, however unfair. (Tsoukas referred to the process as "governmental management by embarrassment".) The retelling of the story of UK post-war government created a consistent alternative model which provided the context for the externally generated information. Without this consistent alternative model, it would have been possible for the recipients to reject the data presented to them. Tsoukas also cites Gregory Bateson: "Information is a difference that makes a difference". The externally generated differences, the league tables and clear-up rates were information rather than just data, because of the difference they made to the autopoietic systems they perturbed.

Sharing responsibility for passing the buck

dialogue

The London Borough of Southwark reorganised its housing department using a process which sounds very much like Tsoukas' prescription for reforming a resistant social system, according to John Kay's account in *The Financial Times* ('Sharing Responsibility for Passing the Buck', 23 October 1995). Nineteen neighbourhood offices were created and 'pestered' with information about how well they were doing vis-à-vis each other and other local government agencies. Southwark also

fitness landscape

made all the comparative data publicly available. Southwark was soon processing housing benefit data faster than any other London Borough except Kensington and Chelsea. Southwark's achievement is also a good example of Kauffman's 'patch-based' improvement.

Communicating in organisations

dialogue

Autopoiesis tells us that people are only interested in what they are interested in. So we have a paradox: if we wish to **talk** effectively with staff we must start by **listening** effectively in order to discover their interests. Most so-called communication in organisations is better thought of as 'talking down' from the top to the bottom of the organisation.

When a campaign is started in recognition of communication problems, it is sometimes called a 'communications offensive'. It may well be the latter; it is unlikely to be the former.

Communication with autopoiesis in mind

dialogue

Dialogue (see 'dialogue' in 'Landscapes of Possibility') is an approach to communication which is very much in harmony with the concept of autopoiesis.

Here are some ideas on how to communicate with autopoiesis in mind:

- **start by listening** – identify the interests of your target 'systems'
- **realise that communication isn't just sending a message, it's a process** – establish resonance over a series of interactions
- **tune the communication to suit the self-interests of the systems** – catch their attention with something new: the input must not be too dissonant or it will

be rejected; nor too 'samey' or it will be ignored. It must be a 'difference that makes a difference' to them

- **develop a consistent alternative model** – another way of describing their reality.

For example, if the issue is written response times for telephone queries in a firm, there are a number of possible sources of information. Research will be needed to locate information and establish a plausible context for it. Suitable information might be comparisons of written response times for queries in other departments of the firm, or written response times for queries to similar firms. The potential for embarrassment must be present.

Autopoiesis clues

We are all aware of autopoiesis to some extent. When we say, 'You only hear what you want to hear', we are acknowledging its power. Some managers rely on ideas like, 'Make them think it's their own idea'. When we say to a friend, 'If I were you...' we are attempting to influence an autopoietic system.

New forms of communication in networks – RBC

The Xerox corporation is using receiver-based communication (RBC) to improve continuously the work of its repair teams. Each worker has a walkie-talkie which is on all the time, carrying messages, just like the radio in a taxi. When a repair worker hears something relevant to a problem they are interested in, they will pay close attention. In this way, improvements spread rapidly across the group. This communication-based strategy goes with the grain of autopoiesis rather than against it.

receiver-based communication (RBC)

Cross-references
dialogue, complex adaptive systems, system, memes, receiver-based communication (RBC)

References

Gregory Bateson, *Steps Towards an Ecology of Mind*, Ballantine, 1972, ISBN 0 345 33291 1

Stuart Kaufmann, 'Order for Free', in John Brockman, *The Third Culture*, Simon & Schuster, 1995, ISBN 0 684 80359 3

Humberto Maturana and Francisco Varela, *The Tree Of Knowledge: the Biological Roots of Human Understanding*, Shambhala Publications, 1987, ISBN 0 87773 642 1

Michael McMaster, *The Intelligence Advantage: Organising for Complexity*, Butterworth-Heinemann, 1996, ISBN 0 7506 9792 X

Tsoukas, H. and Papoulias, D., 'Understanding Social Reforms: a Conceptual Analysis', *Journal of the Operational Research Society*, 47, 1996, pp 853-863

Mindtools for navigating complexity

"Just as you cannot do very much carpentry with your bare hands, there is not much thinking you can do with your bare brain."

Bo Dahlbom and Lars-Erik Janlert

The 'complexity perspective'

Navigating complexity requires making a fundamental shift in the way we understand our world and the way we relate to it. Complexity theory offers no quick fixes, no new answers to the old managerial and organisational problems: instead it offers us new questions which can produce powerful new insights and distinctions. This section offers some hints and tips to help you adopt the 'complexity perspective' without falling into the 'easy answers' trap. These 'mindtools' can be summed up in two imperatives:

* be a different thinker
* be a better learner.

Be a different thinker

Human organisations are complicated: look inside and you'll find a chaos of competing priorities and principles, with new initiatives being introduced almost at random, using huge amounts of resources often for little apparent gain. Now think about a wood. Concealed beneath those rotting leaves and thickets of weeds is an exquisitely complex system in which hundreds of species are sustained through billions of interdependent relationships. Thinking inside the logic of a wood challenges our perspective: it invites us to focus on processes rather than events. Our attention is drawn to **relationships** rather than individuals, to **patterns** and rhythms rather than beginnings and ends. Keen gardeners will understand this intuitively – but why wait until you retire to learn from living systems?

Think relationships

Look inside an ant hill. A single ant only lives three to four days, yet a colony of thousands persists – a series of vast, patterned flows of interactions responding superbly to its changing environment. Think about your organisation. What would happen if **every** job was done by temps who only stayed three days? We can't directly copy the ant's relationship-building trick, but we can use our own special social communication tool – language – to help us mimic their agility.

complex adaptive systems, dialogue, possibility space

Alan Webber describes how at Xerox Business Services (XBS), if you ask 'What's a shared vision?', they don't show you a laminated plastic card full of inspirational slogans, they tell you, 'It's the way we talked with each other when we got together in Orlando'. They are pointing to dynamic processes – relationships, not words on paper – 'talking', 'getting together', 'the way we...' XBS bring their staff and customers together in huge groups (from 120 upwards) because they believe that shared vision is a living thing, part of the organic system of the organisation. They learn how to build relationships and how to have effective conversations. It's a conscious use of language, both verbal and non-verbal, to bind people together in the 'social glue' – the very reason that language evolved in the first place, according to Robin Dunbar.

dialogue

Think community

John Seely Brown, chief scientist at Xerox, describes how a 'Community of Practice' was created amongst copier repair staff. Xerox hired anthropologists who discovered that the swapping of 'war stories' – stories in which a 'hero' defeated the 'worst–ever problem' – was a key part of the knowledge exchange for the repair staff. If you don't honour this process, says Brown, they'll tell stories about the worst-ever training event instead. The introduction of the walkie-talkies greatly improved the sharing of learning, but something more was needed: a process of community-based knowledge **refinement**. A process was developed in which 'authors' of 'tips' made suggestions which were vetted by 'editors' and 'referees' before being rejected or accepted. The staff **refused bonuses** as a reward for contributing to the 'tips case base': what they valued was an 'internal good', the recognition of their peers in their community.

receiver-based communication (RBC)

autopoiesis

Think network

This isn't the traditional corporate database: instead it is a messy network of living distributed knowledge. But the knowledge doesn't live in the computer: rather it is **embodied** in the relationships between the members of the community. By systematically applying complexity concepts to the development of knowledge, Xerox are creating an enabling structure which fosters learning relationships: a 'Community of Practice'. John Seely Brown says that 'the web' – meaning the Xerox intranet – **'leverages the small efforts of the many to drive learning and innovation'**. Forget networking as a synonym for a 'power lunch', think of networking as 'working with relationships'. According to the inquiry report, knowledge hoarding, lack of trust and weak relationships were key factors in the Barings Bank fiasco. The power of a network can be summed up neatly in the Fast Company slogan: **no one is as smart as everyone.**

Think pattern management

The recent business obsession with results, the 'bottom line', has seriously damaged the ability of many organisations to understand and adapt to the patterns of change in their environment. Belatedly, companies are realising that intellectual capital is more than just a buzzword, as massive layoffs lead to a massive loss of expertise in the form of the collective know-how of managers and workforce. Managers at Xerox know that their organisational adaptability and agility come from the little contributions of the many, not just from the big ideas of the top few. Ten years ago, John Harvey-Jones described his role as a CEO as "holding up a mirror to the organisation". Now complexity theory enables us to understand the key principle operating here: honouring emergence in a complex adaptive system.

Recent computer simulations by Chris Langton's team at the Santa Fe´ Institute have shown that if you want to change a complex adaptive system from the outside (a task comparable to herding cats), you have to 'create a representation of the interactions in the system and enable the independent agents in the system to communicate about the representation'. In the simulations without this representation, the 'agents' simply ignored the outside influences, treating them as mere perturbations. In human terms, you can't simply manipulate a team or a department from outside by telling them what to do. Humans are sense-making organisms: therefore you have to allow them to make sense of the task for themselves by giving them information about the combined results of their actions, and enabling them to talk about it. This is the nitty-gritty of "holding up a mirror to the organisation".

Some tips: go for lots of frequent small changes rather than a few big ones because the results of small changes can be fed back quickly to the group and it's less traumatic for them. Nobody likes late feedback; they'll say 'Why didn't you tell me earlier?' The more rapid this 'iteration', the faster the learning and adaptation to produce the desired result. At the start, nobody will have a precise idea what is needed, but in just the same way that you can navigate a ship by making several small course corrections – 'left a bit, steady, right a bit' – you can manage the emergence of a pattern, an attractor. Each time the emergent pattern is fed back to the team, things become a little bit clearer: 'We're looking for something like this or this, not that'. It's the same methodology that Mother Nature has used to create all life on this planet – selection of the fittest. We can sum up pattern management as 'managing the internal environment of the organisation to enable knowledge development and application'.

attractor

Be a better learner

You can't be a better learner if you're not already learning: only you can be responsible for your learning. The more you do it, the faster and better you get – making more connections, deepening your understanding. Learning works best when it's 'self-organised' in your personal 'zone of complexity'. If you agree with Christine Turner at Xerox Business Services (XBS) that "learning is your only chance to keep up with change", here's what you need to do.

self-organisation, the 'edge of chaos', increasing returns and lock-in

Be a better listener

'We tried to tell you, but you weren't listening' is the habitual lament from workers involved in improvement initiatives. Seek out opportunities to listen. And remember: **dialogue** is not discussion, it's about reflection and multiple perspectives, not 'one best way'.

dialogue

Be a volunteer

When you are a volunteer, you are just the same as everybody else; the power and status you have at work is left behind for the day. You could be part of a team that planted a thousand trees in a morning, working alongside a group of children, their parents and a whole spectrum of other people who are all there for the same reason you are – to give their time freely to something they believe in. It can give you a whole new perspective on 'organisation' and 'work'.

network and hierarchy

Be a wider reader

Broaden your range of inputs: read outside your field, read some fiction or even some science fiction. This will help to build up those 'thinking muscles' you don't normally use. And when you broaden your reading, here's some 'homework'. Look at the strangest things you've read and think how they might relate to the work of your organisation. Edward de Bono describes this as a "provocative operation". When he tells us that "There may not be a reason for saying something until after it has been said", it applies equally to what you have just read.

possibility space

Be a post-modern apprentice

At every opportunity ask, 'What can I learn here? What can this person or these people teach me?' as if it is a privilege to have a learning opportunity – which of course it is. Specifically, let someone younger tutor you in something they know more about than you: it could be your children, or your newest or youngest member of staff. It's a kind of lifetime apprenticeship: you acknowledge that others know things you don't, and commit yourself to learning from them; but what you learn is up to you.

perspectives

 References

Edward de Bono, *de Bono's Thinking Course*, BBC Publications, 1994, ISBN 0 563 37073 4

John Seely Brown, 'Innovation and the Social Mind', presentation to the Complexity and Technology: Organising for Innovation conference, London, 10/11 March 1997

'Mapping and Transferring Knowledge' in *Bulletpoint*, Issue 37, January 1997

Bo Dahlbom and Lars-Erik Janlert quoted in Daniel Dennett, *Kinds of Minds*, Weidenfeld and Nicholson, 1996, ISBN 0 297 81546 6

Chris Langton and associates, recent research quoted by Michael Lissack in personal communication, Plexis seminar, London, 3/4 June 1997

Alan M. Webber, 'XBS Learns to Grow' in *The New Rules of Business*, Fast Company, Summer 1997

Next steps

The sequel to this book is in preparation under the working title *Living Complexity*. It will introduce a further set of new science concepts and learning methodologies. The book will demonstrate how pioneering organisations have developed new tools for thought and action that are enabling them not just to navigate complexity, but to adapt creatively to it. New science concepts will include:

- evolutionary psychology and anthropology
- linguistics
- new thinking on leadership
- theories of cognition and learning.

Applications, illustrated with narrative cases and anecdotes from both the private and public sector, will include:

- enabling a reorganised top team to develop effective skills for listening, visioning and action
- rapid and effective community and stakeholder consultation with thousands of individuals
- unlocking creativity in a team of consultants.

Update your Navigating Complexity resources
Subscribe to the Navigating Complexity bulletin at: navlist@mail.com. You can also visit the Navigating Complexity website at: www.indsoc.co.uk/navcom

The Industrial Society offers courses and consultancy on issues in organisational and individual learning. Visit the website: www.indsoc.co.uk

Epilogue: Tools for thought

I was first introduced to complexity theory by Mitchell Waldrop's book *Complexity*. About half-way into it I had a revelation about the nature of organisations: it was as if I could see the whole scheme of things, and not just see it, actually grasp it. I could see how everything fitted together, I could see where the potential was and what needed to be done and I was overwhelmed with a profound depression. I could see in my mind's eye the vast glowing network of possibilities and yet I felt that I could do absolutely nothing about it. So I put the book away and went back to focusing on the work at hand.

About a year later, I packed Waldrop as holiday reading. I had just been assigned to a new team at work and felt that there might be some possibilities for our project in the book. The next week I found myself at a converted farmhouse in the Languedoc explaining complex adaptive systems to my fellow guests. This was the start of my personal 'navigation in complexity' and it was also a return to something else that I had put away: one of my core beliefs. I had held at bay for twenty years the idea that I could do something to make the world a better place. Now I would accept the challenge. The warm response which has greeted the earlier version of this book encourages me to believe that I may yet be able to contribute to this goal.

I tell this story not just because it may be of personal interest but because in some respects it illustrates the difficulties you will face as you start 'navigating complexity'. As Daniel Goleman reminds us, our thinking is profoundly influenced by our emotions. You may have to wrestle with your feelings as you try to relate these strange ideas to the realities of your organisation. Think carefully about who you talk to and choose your moments wisely.

I will leave the final words to C.H. Waddington, whose book *Tools for Thought* was the inspiration for this one:

> *"... what we are really confronting is a complex of complexes. This has been called the World Problematique. It is a formidable situation; but this is what the world is like at the present time. It is for this reason that the development of adequate tools for thought about complex systems is so overwhelmingly important."*

Arthur Battram,
Greece and London, June-July 1997

 ## References

Daniel Goleman, *Emotional Intelligence*, Bloomsbury, 1996, ISBN 0 7475 2625 7

C.H. Waddington, *Tools for Thought*, Paladin, 1977

Waddington's book, written in 1975, was the the first to introduce concepts such as attractors, fitness landscapes and lock-in to a general audience, predating the Santa Fé Institute by twenty years. It is still an unparalleled introduction to thinking about complex systems.

Special offer

If you enjoyed *Navigating Complexity*, and are interested in both practical applications of complexity theory and deeper insights into the nature of systems, you may be interested in the *Complexity and Learning* bundle from The Improvement and Development Agency, containing the following items:

Navigating complexity wallchart

Summarising the key concepts explored in *Navigating Complexity* **(full colour A2 poster)**.

Self-organising for Success: Creating a Learning Culture

A 'turnaround' success story in which a struggling group of public sector staff escapes a vicious cycle of rising complaints and dissatisfaction. They become a powerful and productive team by using the principles of organisational learning, dialogue, and emergence. The approach used creates 'learning from customers' by combining partnership and stakeholder ideas with complexity theory concepts (such as attractors, 'edge of chaos', and coevolution) and elements of the 'Five Disciplines' of Peter Senge. **(A5, 40 pages)**

The Simple and the Complex: the Patterns of Life

This often poetic and profound work offers insights into the basic patterns of systems as diverse as companies, ant colonies, traffic jams, teams and the learning processes in your mind. By appreciating the hidden similarities of different systems, we can deepen our understanding of the systems in which we live and work. The booklet offers a unique perspective on the nature of systems theory and the language of systems thinking, examining the key concepts of system, pattern, structure, process, independent behaviour and emergence. **(A5, 36 pages)**

Ordering the complexity and learning bundle

Photocopy this page from the book, complete the form with your delivery details and send it to:

Publications Dept, IDA, 76-86 Turnmill St, London, UK, EC1M 5QU or fax it to: +44 (0)20 7296 6523. Please allow 28 days for delivery.

The bundle is available for £14 plus £1 for postage and packing (while stocks last), UK only. (Phone +44 (0)20 7296 6512 for international p&p charges.) Please make cheques or international money orders payable to The Improvement and Development Agency.

Name ....

Organisation ....

Address ....

....

....

Postcode ....

Tel ....

Fax ....

Credit card payments

❏ Visa   ❏ Mastercard   Expiry date............................

Card holder's name ....

Card number..

Card holder's signature...

Index

Index